SAVAGE STANDARDS

Copyright © 2025 by Chad McMillan

Published by Four Rivers Media

All rights reserved. No portion of this book may be reproduced, stored in a retrieval system, or transmitted in any form or by any means—electronic, mechanical, photocopy, recording, scanning, or other—except for brief quotations in critical reviews or articles, without prior written permission of the author.

For foreign and subsidiary rights, contact the author.

Cover design by: Sara Young & Todd Petelle
Cover photo by: Andrew van Tilborgh

ISBN: 978-1-964794-95-2   1 2 3 4 5 6 7 8 9 10

Printed in the United States of America

WHATS BEING SAID ABOUT
SAVAGE STANDARDS

I've had the honor of calling Chad McMillan one of my closest friends for over thirty years. Across three decades of friendship, ministry, deep conversations, and laughter, one thing has remained constant: Chad's ability to inspire. I've often heard it said that boredom is the rust of a lack of inspiration, and whenever I feel that rust creeping into my ministry or creative work, Chad shows up with a spark. He doesn't just think outside the box; he sets the whole box on fire and builds something better from the ashes.

In *Savage Standards*, Chad pours out the raw, hard-earned wisdom that can only come from life lived honestly and intensely. These aren't idealistic musings or trendy self-help platitudes. They're forged through experience—the kind that wounds you, wakes you up, and ultimately redefines you. Chad didn't write this book from a safe distance; he lived it. And we have the privilege to glean from that journey.

This is a manifesto for those ready to quit negotiating with dysfunction and finally claim their voice. It's bold. It's disruptive. And it's necessary. In a world that constantly asks you to blur your boundaries to keep the peace, *Savage Standards* dares you to hold the line. Not from bitterness, but from clarity and courage.

Read it slowly. Wrestle with it. Let it wreck your passivity and awaken your resolve. I did, and I'm better for it.

—Dr. Matthew Hester
Pastor
Author of *The Rorschach God*
Host of *The Kingdom Is for Everyone*

Savage Standards is an honest and clarifying playbook for business and creative teams who want to foster healthy and fruitful boundaries with their clients—while not sacrificing creative instinct—and start building a business foundation that actually honors them. Chad McMillan cuts through the noise with a hard-learned clarity, ruthless prioritization, and thoughtful, humane approach to scaling your business. It's a bold, precise, and surprisingly compassionate read. It gives you the framework and courage to elevate the creative output, win better clients, and build a lasting business. Enjoy the ride. . . . READ IT, SWALLOW THE RULES, SET THE BOUNDARIES, and then watch everything else that doesn't deserve your attention fall away.

—Mike Pereyo
Founder, OOBE

SAVAGE STANDARDS
A BOUNDARY-SETTING MANIFESTO

RULES FOR LIFE
AND BUSINESS THAT
DON'T FLINCH,
FOLD, OR
~~F*CK~~ AROUND

CHAD MCMILLAN

Dedication

To my wife, Cami—*the calm in my storm, the steady hand on my back, and the heart behind everything I do. Your love, patience, and unshakable belief in me have carried me through more than you'll ever know. I hit the jackpot with you.*

To my kids, Sam and Bella—*you are my why. Watching you grow, dream, and become who you are meant to be is the greatest joy of my life. This book, and the life it came from, is all for you.*

And to my mom, Janet, *who left this world in 2024 but has never left my heart. Your grit, courage, and relentless work ethic shaped the man I am. You showed me how to stand tall, even when life tries to knock me down. I miss you every day, but your light still leads the way. This one's for all of you.*

CONTENTS

Foreword xi
Acknowledgments xiii
Introduction 15
RULE 1. Don't Work with Assholes 21
RULE 2. Relationships Don't Fit on a Spreadsheet 35
RULE 3. Budgets Don't Define Brilliance 47
RULE 4. People Do Business with People 55
RULE 5. Passion > Perfection 67
RULE 6. DEI—Do Everything Intentionally 81
RULE 7. Everything Is an Experiment 89
RULE 8. Act Like It, Attract Like It 103
RULE 9. Busy Is Bullsh*t 111
RULE 10. Skip the Problem 121
RULE 11. Pick Up the Damn Phone 131
RULE 12. If It's Not a Hell Yes, It's a Hell No 141
RULE 13. Stop Trying to Prove Your Worth 151
RULE 14. Protect Your Power Source 165
RULE 15. Your Business Is Not Your Identity 179
Conclusion 187

FOREWORD

In the ever-evolving landscape of marketing, clarity and conviction are rare commodities. At X-Agency, we've built our reputation on cutting through the noise, and much of that comes from the unapologetic vision and values laid out in this book. I've had the privilege of witnessing firsthand how these guiding principles have shaped not only the DNA of our agency but have also fueled real, measurable results for our clients. They're not just theories; they're an ethos that we live, breathe, and execute every day. This book isn't a collection of abstract ideas; it's a blueprint forged in the crucible of real-world experience. It's a testament to the power of bold thinking and decisive action in an industry that often favors the safe and familiar. But what sets this book apart is the man behind it. Chad isn't just my business partner; he's someone I've built big dreams with. Over years of long strategy sessions, chaotic launches, early wins, late-night pivots, and the kind of honest conversations most people avoid, I've seen him stay fiercely loyal to the truth. He's the kind of thinker who challenges comfort zones and invites bolder action. Working alongside Chad means being in constant proximity to big ideas, sharp insight, and a rare kind of leadership that's equal parts guts and heart. This book is an extension of who he is—straight-shooting, insightful, and willing to call bullshit on anything that dilutes creative integrity. It's a roadmap for anyone who wants to stop playing small in business and in life. So, if you're ready to draw the line and find out what it really takes to build something meaningful, welcome. You're in good company.

—Brooke Barlow
Co-Founder, X-Agency

ACKNOWLEDGMENTS

This book would still be sitting in a Google Doc titled "Maybe Someday" if it weren't for a handful of people who kept me focused, grounded, and just the right amount of unhinged.

First and foremost, to Brooke—my business partner, my voice of reason, my co-creator in all things strategy and sanity. Thank you for relentlessly keeping me in line, for helping me turn chaos into clarity, and for never letting me run from the hard parts. You've seen every version of this book (and me)—the good, the gritty, and the grumbly—and somehow still chose to lean in and help shape it. These rules wouldn't exist without you, and I sure as hell wouldn't be living them without you either.

To my friends and family, who have endured years of my passionate rants, my late-night brainstorms, and my absolute refusal to take the easy road. Thank you. You've supported me when I doubted myself, laughed with me when I needed it most, and reminded me why this work matters. Your encouragement, patience, and love have been my fuel.

And finally, to anyone who's ever believed in me more than I believed in myself. This book is for you. You know who you are. I hope I made you proud.

Now let's go build something that doesn't suck.

—Chad

Savagestandards.com

INTRODUCTION

First things first: **This book is a line in the sand. It isn't a how-to manual, but a hard stop.**

It took me a long time to put all of my thoughts together for this manuscript. Mostly because I thought these principles were common sense and didn't need any narrative. What I found when talking to a lot of other colleagues in business (and in life) struggling with these very same issues is that these "common sense" principles ... aren't actually all that common.

I didn't write this book to get a speaking gig. I didn't write it to look smart on social media. I didn't write it because the world needs another over-engineered business book filled with TED Talk swagger and bullet points about "grit."

I wrote this because, after decades in the trenches, in boardrooms, Zoom calls, late-night concept sprints, and way too many emails saying, "Can you make the logo bigger?" I hit a wall. Actually, I didn't just hit it. I slammed into it face-first, dragging a team of talented, overworked people with me.

I'm a creative. A builder. A strategist. I've worked in big agencies and small studios, and eventually, I built my own thing alongside a business partner who understood my struggle more than anyone. Someone who's helped me refine the points in this book over all the time we've partnered together.

Over the years, we've worked with companies in nearly every industry: startups with nothing but hustle, legacy brands with more baggage than vision, ministries with as much determination as their mission, founders full of fire, and executives full of excuses.

We've helped businesses launch, scale, reimagine, and survive. We've written decks that closed million-dollar deals, branding strategies that ignited growth, and messaging that brought clarity to chaos.

But we've also seen a lot of wreckage. False starts. Bad hires. Half-baked pivots. And more "we'll circle back on that" than I care to admit.

And we've seen the pattern. Every time a business fell apart, it wasn't because of the logo. It wasn't because of the campaigns. It wasn't even because of the market.

It was the people.

The wrong clients. The wrong teams. The wrong energy. The wrong motives.

People who wanted a shortcut, not a solution. People who thought hiring others meant buying control. People chasing clout, cash, and "crush it" culture at the expense of sanity, substance, and soul.

I wrote this book because I've lived through all of it, and I'm done pretending it's just "part of the job."

This book is a crowbar. A manifesto. A middle finger to burnout disguised as ambition. It's the result of two and a half decades of hard-earned clarity and even harder decisions.

I've worked with brilliant collaborators and walked away from lucrative contracts. I've watched teams around me shine, and I've watched them crumble under the weight of toxic requirements and unrealistic expectations.

We weren't broken because of a lack of talent.

We were bleeding out because we let the wrong people in the room. And that's on us.

So, we drew a line.

We fired the soul-suckers. We stopped negotiating with narcissists. We got clear on our values and ruthless about our borders. And somewhere in all that burn-it-down energy, we found something sacred: Our sanity. Our creativity. Our actual joy.

This book is about that line and what happens when you decide to stop tolerating the things that drain you and open up to the things that feed you. It's about building a business that reflects your values instead of eroding them. It's about remembering that success isn't just about growth. It's about alignment and integrity.

Each chapter is a rule.

Not some inspirational fluff. Not recycled startup wisdom. These are the rules we wrote when we got tired of other people writing them for us. Each one is a real-ass rule we learned the hard way. A rule we now live by.

This is for the ones building something with weight. With meaning. With fire.

For the creative who's done with clients who treat every brainstorm like a hostage negotiation.

For the founder who's exhausted by the endless compromises and client red flags they ignored—again.

For the manager tired of turning their job into a full-time motivational seminar on a slightly above-average salary.

For the team leader who knows that protecting your people is the most profitable move you'll ever make.

For the business owner wrestling with their ideas just as much as their doubts.

For the burnt-out high performer who's starting to wonder if being "in demand" is just another trap.

For any pastor, priest, or non-profit leader who's had their passion challenged so many times, it makes them question their faith in humanity.

Even though I've written this from the perspective of a business owner, it applies to every person who's building something right now: A career. A business. A team. A product. A mission. Or an organization.

This is for anyone ready to stop playing by everyone else's rules and start building with intention.

Because here's the deal: **If you don't set the rules, someone else will.** And chances are, their rules will bury your joy, your patience, and your peace under a pile of soul-draining work.

If you're not careful, your profession will become a prison.

This book is how you bust the hell out.

It's about SAVAGE STANDARDS.

When lines are crossed, limits tested, your work is undervalued, or your boundaries are constantly violated, you need a reset.

This book isn't about playing nice, fitting in, or keeping the peace while you quietly crumble. It's about setting standards so damn clear they feel like a brick wall to the things that don't respect them.

This book isn't a collection of polite suggestions or gentle encouragement. It's a boundary-setting manifesto—a blueprint for what happens when you stop tolerating the intolerable. When you stop overexplaining your worth. When you stop playing by the rules in rooms that never respected you in the first place. Consider this your official permission slip to stop putting up with bullsh*t.

No footnotes, no fine print, no caveats.

Each rule in this book is a direct response to the real-world fallout of letting the wrong people or the wrong motivations call the shots. These aren't theories. They're scars. Hard-won lessons. Every rule is a line we've had to draw—sometimes, in pencil, sometimes, in blood.

Your standards are your strategy. They're the line between a business you run and a business that runs you ragged. They're the difference between a life you resent and one you love waking up to.

It's about building a life, a business, and a mindset that refuses to flinch, fold, or f*ck around when it comes to your energy, your passion, and your purpose.

It's about refusing to beg for scraps of respect from clients, bosses, or anyone else who treats your time or your talents like a commodity.

It's about realizing that every time you lower your standards, you train the world to keep testing your limits. And every time you raise them, you reclaim your power.

It's about setting your standards so high they scare off the wrong people before they even get to your door.

Low standards don't keep the peace. They keep you stuck. And high standards don't make you difficult. They make you dangerous to mediocrity.

If your standards don't make you or others around you uncomfortable, then you've set the bar too low.

This book is your warning AND your armor.

It's the energy you carry into every conversation where your time, your experience, or your expertise are on the line.

It's not about being reckless. It's about being resolute.

You don't build a great business by playing it safe. You build it by knowing where your line is and having the guts to hold it when it counts. You build it by letting people find out what happens when they test your values and underestimate your standards.

This is a challenge to every people-pleaser, over-deliverer, boundary-blurrer, and burnout survivor who's had enough. It's a call to step fully into the version of you who knows what's worth protecting.

So, if you've ever asked:

How do I stop working with people who drain me?
How do I build a business that reflects who I really am?
How do I set my standards without burning it all down?

This is your answer.

If you're tired of tiptoeing around chaos, apologizing for your ideas, or letting hustle culture convince you that exhaustion is a badge of honor, good. This book is for you.

You set the rule. You hold the line.

So, crack the spine. Let the sugarcoating melt. Get honest. Get angry. Get free.

Fire a few clients (mentally or actually). Reclaim your voice. Rework the terms. Rewrite the playbook. Change the game.

Let's build something with backbone. Something honest. Something sharp.

Let's kick the damn door open and build something you actually love . . . one rule at a time.

Make these your SAVAGE STANDARDS.

RULE 1

DON'T WORK WITH ASSHOLES

ONE RULE TO RULE THEM ALL

There it is. Bold. Blunt. Maybe a little jarring. But it's absolutely essential.

Make this your first rule.

This isn't just a cheeky motto or something we slap on a coffee mug or t-shirt. It's a cornerstone of how we do business, build relationships, and sleep soundly at night. "We don't work with assholes" may sound irreverent, but it's one of the most important and strategic decisions we've ever made.

THE ASSHOLE TAX: YOU'RE ALREADY PAYING IT

Let's be clear: Assholes come with hidden fees. This isn't a hypothetical expense. You're already paying it—in time, energy, morale, and lost opportunity. The Asshole Tax is real, and it's embedded deep in the operational costs of every business that hasn't learned to say no to the wrong people.

You know exactly who we're talking about.

It's the client who insists on another "quick call" at 6:45 p.m. on a Friday and then shows up ten minutes late or cancels after you've waited.

It's the one who questions your invoices like you're trying to scam them out of all their money, while conveniently forgetting the extra time your team spent saving their last-minute screw-up.

TOXIC PEOPLE DON'T JUST HURT YOUR BUSINESS; THEY MESS WITH YOUR HEAD.

It's the one who treats your employees like servers at a bad restaurant—barking orders, shifting blame, and making every interaction feel like a performance review where only they have the answer key.

And it's not just clients. The Asshole Tax shows up in team members and vendors, too. You know the ones: the brilliant-but-toxic employee who turns every meeting into a therapy session, derails momentum with drama, and leaves a trail of sighs behind them. Or the vendor who's always almost done but mysteriously disappears whenever accountability shows up. They might deliver just enough to keep their job or contract, but the emotional overhead they create costs more than any invoice ever will. You're not paying them for their talent—you're subsidizing their chaos.

We didn't even know we were paying for it—we just finally started noticing the bill. Here's what they cost you, even if you think it will get better:

1) They Erode Morale

Nothing tanks a team's spirit faster than feeling unappreciated or, worse, disrespected. The moment your team realizes that toxic behavior is tolerated in the name of a paycheck, they begin to check out. First emotionally, then physically.

Your best people—the ones who raise their hands in meetings, stay curious, and truly care—won't stick around to be collateral damage in your tolerance of dysfunction. They'll leave. And they'll be right to.

Even those who stay will start doing just enough to avoid conflict. The sense of ownership disappears. Innovation slows. Cynicism creeps in. All because one person was allowed to run roughshod over your values.

2) They Suck Up Disproportionate Resources

You'll spend 80 percent of your account management energy on 20 percent of your worst clients. That's the rule, whether you like it or not.

You want to know the first way to tell if they're a toxic person? They over-communicate when it's unnecessary and under-communicate when it matters most.

They burn out managers, tie up your team, require extra steps "just in case," and generally create a gravity well that pulls your entire organization off balance.

While good people are humming along—collaborative, respectful, efficient—you're wasting valuable internal cycles chasing an ever-moving target that never seems satisfied.

3) They Damage Your Reputation

Assholes have a way of creating chaos in public. They demand the world, then turn around and say you underdelivered. They rewrite the story of the engagement to make themselves the victim.

They leave scorched-earth emails. They leave one-star reviews with no context. And worse? They talk, especially if they're influential. One toxic person with a loud voice can sow enough doubt in your market to undo years of solid work.

The reputation hit doesn't stop at the front door either. Prospective employees notice when a company has a revolving door. Talent will sniff out toxicity like a bloodhound. Your organization will suffer, your pipeline will slow, and you won't even realize you've become radioactive until it's too late.

4) They Undermine Your Confidence

Here's the part no one talks about: **Toxic people don't just hurt your business; they mess with your head.** They second-guess your judgment, poke holes in your process, and gaslight your instincts.

Over time, you begin to wonder if maybe you're the problem. Maybe your team isn't up to the task. Or maybe you do need to discount more or say yes faster.

This is the most dangerous cost of all: the erosion of your professional confidence. Because once that's gone, everything else begins to wobble.

5) They Block Better Business

Every minute you spend managing a difficult person is a minute you're not spending building stronger partnerships with great ones. It's a minute you're not investing in better processes, mentoring your team, or thinking strategically about your next move. It's a minute less of your peace.

Bad individuals crowd out the good. They clog the pipeline, hog internal resources, and blur your vision. They make you reactive instead of proactive . . . busy instead of effective.

And worst of all? They teach you to settle. To tolerate what should be intolerable.

THE FINAL INVOICE . . .

So, what's the final bill?

It looks like lower retention, higher stress, missed opportunities, team burnout, brand risk, and a culture that quietly asks, "Is this really worth it?"

That's the Asshole Tax.

And once you see it clearly, you realize that no client is worth paying it.

THE POWER OF THE "NO": HOW WE STOPPED BEING PEOPLE-PLEASERS AND STARTED SLEEPING AGAIN

Let's get real: **Saying "No" is hard.** It goes against years of professional conditioning, our childhood need for approval, and the little entrepreneurial voice in our heads that whispers, "Don't blow it. This could be the big one!"

In the early days, we said yes to everything. Yes to every prospect, every project, every red-flag-waving client who claimed to be "fast-moving and results-driven" (translation: chaotic messes that are allergic to deadlines). We convinced ourselves we were "hustling," "paying dues," and "earning our stripes." But what we were really doing was slow-dripping poison into our company's bloodstream.

> ## AS SOON AS WE STARTED SAYING NO TO THE WRONG PEOPLE, THE RIGHT ONES STARTED SHOWING UP.

Here's how bad it got:

One of our best designers, who was an actual creative unicorn with the patience of a monk, left a Zoom call with a client, turned off her camera, and audibly muttered, "I'm going to fake my own death."

Our seasoned project manager developed a nervous eye twitch that seemed to activate every time the client's name hit her inbox.

And we found ourselves rewriting entire scopes of work at 11:57 p.m. because a client "had a new vision" that came to him in a hot yoga class.

That's when we drew the line.

Not a dotted line. Not a pencil line. A thick, black, permanent marker line that said, *No more.*

Saying "No" Was the Best Business Decision We Ever Made

We thought turning clients away would tank our revenue. We braced for a dry spell, a dip, and maybe even a sad email to our landlord explaining that exposure and experience don't pay rent.

But a funny thing happened: As soon as we started saying no to the wrong people, the right ones started showing up. People who respected boundaries. People who understood value. People who didn't treat our team like overcaffeinated interns running a group project.

And guess what?

Our work improved because we weren't constantly firefighters in damage control.

Our team got happier—like, genuinely happy. Smiling-on-Zoom, taking-vacations, suggesting-ideas-again happy. It was great. Our profits grew, all because we stopped spending our time negotiating with emotional terrorists over a $200 change order.

Turns out, the word "no" is like a GPS recalibration. It reroutes you away from drama and toward meaningful, healthy, sustainable work.

"No" Isn't Negative. It's Protective.

Here's the thing most people misunderstand: **Saying no doesn't make you arrogant, difficult, or ungrateful. It makes you wise.**

It's like dating. Just because someone likes you doesn't mean you owe them a relationship. Some people are just not your match. Maybe they're too disorganized. Maybe they don't trust the process. Maybe they make everything feel like a group project led by a drunk raccoon.

Whatever the reason, the "no" is your defense against misalignment, misery, and management PTSD.

It's how you protect your process, your people, and your peace.

A FINAL NOTE ON KINDNESS

Don't be an asshole either.

We're not in the business of being jerks. Quite the opposite. We believe in being generous, collaborative, and radically helpful. But kindness without boundaries is a fast track to burnout. And boundaries without enforcement? That's just wishful thinking.

Saying no isn't about being harsh. It's about being clear. And clarity is one of the kindest things you can offer.

So, here's to the "no."

To the polite pass. The confident decline. The "thanks but no thanks." To saying goodbye to clients who make you feel like you're walking barefoot through a Lego factory.

Because when you say no to the wrong work, you're really saying yes to the right life.

HOW TO SPOT ONE BEFORE IT'S TOO LATE

Assholes don't always announce themselves in the first meeting. Sometimes, they show up in tailored suits with a charming smile. But red flags tend to flutter early if you know what to look for:

» They talk more than they listen.
» They belittle people when they think no one's watching.
» They haggle over price without respecting value.
» They use urgency as a manipulation tool.
» They name-drop and posture instead of collaborating.

If your gut says, "This might be a nightmare wrapped in a contract," listen to it. Intuition is an incredible survival instinct in business. We'll get more into this in a later chapter.

THE INTERNAL EFFECT: HOW WE FIRED OUR BIGGEST CLIENT AND THE UNIVERSE SENT A THANK-YOU NOTE

If there's one non-negotiable piece of business advice I can give you, it's this: **Protect your people like they're your most valuable asset because they are.**

Clients come and go. Invoices get paid (eventually). Projects wrap. But your team? Your team is the engine, the soul, and the future of your business. And when you let someone mistreat them, even just once, the damage spreads faster than you think.

We learned this the hard way.

The Client We Should've Walked Away from Sooner

They were our biggest account. Like, BIGGEST.

The kind of client whose monthly retainer paid for several salaries and our morning coffee habit. They had the prestige, the brand name, the flash. And at first, we were thrilled. We rolled out the red carpet, staffed the A-team, even stayed late to hit impossible deadlines because, well, "this one matters."

But over time, the shine wore off, and the truth set in. They didn't treat our people like partners. They treated them like punching bags with keyboards.

Creative presentations were met with eyerolls.

Our account manager was routinely talked over, dismissed, and once publicly embarrassed in a meeting for asking a clarifying question.

We had a designer who was incredibly talented, wildly creative, and thoughtful, who walked into a feedback call with confidence and walked out questioning their entire career.

And here's what really stung: They paid us well. They paid on time. They gave us volume. They said all the right things in executive meetings. But behind the scenes, they were slowly poisoning our culture.

We talked about it as a leadership team. A lot. The pros. The cons. And the hit we'd take if we walked.

Then, one day, after another soul-crushing meeting, we just said it: *This isn't worth it. We can't be the kind of company that puts money above everything else we value. We have to live what we say we believe.*

So, we walked.

Respectfully. Professionally. But firmly.

We spoke to the client, ended the contract, and braced for the financial fallout. There was fear. There were concerns. There were a few quiet moments where we stared into space, wondering if we'd just made the dumbest decision of our careers. We prepared ourselves for what the consequences would be financially, but we knew the cost of keeping them would be so much higher.

What happened next?

Two weeks later . . . two weeks . . . we signed a bigger client.

A better client.

They came out of nowhere.

They appreciated the creative process. They trusted our work. They said, "Thank you," in meetings and, "What do you think?" instead of "do it faster." It felt like the universe saw us protecting our peace and whispered back, "Good job. Here's something better."

And our team? They noticed. They felt seen. They realized this wasn't just lip service. We'd actually walk away from real money if it meant protecting them. That changed everything.

Morale went up. Loyalty deepened. And suddenly, we were doing the kind of work we started this company to do in the first place: bold, inspired, and free from emotional landmines.

CULTURE IS A GARDEN, NOT A DEPARTMENT

You can't fake culture. You can't outsource it to HR or just say it's so. Culture is built every day by the decisions you make, especially the hard ones. And nothing says more about what you stand for than the clients you're willing to say goodbye to.

THERE'S ALWAYS ANOTHER CLIENT. BUT THERE'S ONLY ONE OF YOU.

When your team sees that you'll protect them, not just with pep talks, but with real-world action, they give you everything they've got. Their talent. Their trust. Their best ideas.

That's the kind of loyalty you can't buy. You earn it.

So, yeah, walking away from our biggest client was terrifying. But walking away from our values? That would've cost us far more.

There's always another client. But there's only one of you.

TURNING THIS INTO A PRACTICE

If you want to implement this rule in your business, here's how:

» **Define your dealbreakers**. Get your team involved. What's unacceptable behavior? Write it down.

- » **Make it part of your onboarding.** Let prospective clients know how you work and what you value.
- » **Empower your team.** Give them permission to raise red flags without fear.
- » **Be consistent.** Don't cave because someone waves a fat check at you.
- » **Celebrate the good ones.** Celebrate their wins. Brag on great clients to them and to others. Publicly and privately. This is important.

THE HUMAN FACTOR: WE WORK WITH PEOPLE, NOT JUST COMPANIES

At the end of the day, business is human. Every partnership is a relationship. And the best ones are built on mutual respect, patience, trust, and a little laughter.

So, yeah, save yourself a tremendous amount of pain and suffering. If this is the only chapter of this book you read, then make this the one defining rule you won't break.

Don't work with assholes.

This is your war cry. Your standard. Your emotional contract.

THE NO-ASSHOLE ANTHEM (READ IT. REPEAT IT. LIVE IT.)

We don't work with assholes. Not because we're fragile. Not because we can't handle pressure. Not because we expect everyone to bring cookies and gratitude to every meeting.

We don't work with assholes because:
- » Respect is non-negotiable.
- » Kindness is strategic.
- » Toxic energy is expensive. And no amount of money is worth shrinking for.

We protect our team. We protect our time. We protect our creativity like it's oxygen—because it is.

We don't tolerate ego at the expense of empathy. We don't chase chaos dressed as opportunity. We don't explain ourselves to people committed to misunderstanding us. We lead with clarity.

We work with humans, not hurricanes. We build in peace, not panic.

And above all else: **We will never sacrifice our standards to keep the wrong people comfortable.**

So, don't work with assholes. Don't hire them. Don't excuse them. Don't become one just because you're tired, scared, or surrounded by them.

Hold the line. Say the no. Raise the bar. Write the email. Make the call. Walk the f*ck away if you have to. Because when you stop tolerating assholes, you make room for everything real to walk through the door.

And that?

That's the business you came here to build.

RULE 2

RELATIONSHIPS DON'T FIT ON A SPREADSHEET

BUT THAT DOESN'T STOP CFOs FROM TRYING

RELATIONSHIPS DON'T FIT ON A SPREADSHEET

Let's go ahead and say it: We love spreadsheets. They're clean. They're organized. They make us feel in control. They let us color-code chaos. Some of us have even been known to flirt with conditional formatting. (You know who you are.)

But here's the problem: **Not everything that matters fits in a spreadsheet. Especially not relationships.**

Try explaining to a formula why you bent over backwards to help a client hit their product launch. Or why you comped that last hour because their kid was sick, and they forgot to send feedback. Or why you didn't raise rates this year, even though inflation made your office coffee taste like a luxury item.

Try fitting that into a cell marked "ROI."

Spoiler: **You can't. And that's the point.**

HUMANS > FORMULAS

There's something wildly reductive about trying to assign value to human connection in Excel. As if trust can be tracked in a pivot table. As if loyalty has a formula. As if years of collaboration, shared wins, and late-night strategy calls can be distilled down to "Line Item C17—Client Value Over Time."

I'm not saying you should throw your financial models to the wind and start bartering services for good vibes and artisan jam. I'm saying there's a critical part of your business that can't and shouldn't be reduced to metrics alone.

Here's the deal: **Business is personal.**

Anyone who tells you otherwise is either lying or desperately trying to pretend that a spreadsheet didn't just get them ghosted by a long-term client.

THE DANGEROUS MATH OF "JUST BUSINESS"

I've seen it a thousand times.

A company gets a little bigger. A little shinier. They hire a new executive who has all the emotional range of a vending machine. And suddenly, every client interaction is filtered through a cost-benefit analysis spreadsheet written in cold, heartless Arial 10-point font.

Next thing you know, long-standing partners get dropped because "the margin isn't ideal." Projects that bring real joy get cut because they "don't scale." The vendor who pulled all-nighters with you back when your logo was still Comic Sans gets replaced by a cheaper offshore option with no vowels in their name.

And when that company starts to struggle? They can't understand why no one's picking up the phone anymore.

Here's why: Those relationships became a transaction. And people remember that.

WE MEASURE WHAT WE TREASURE

Let's be clear: **The most important metrics in your business aren't always in your dashboard.**

The truth is, some of the things that matter most—the things that truly move the needle long-term—don't show up in your quarterly report. They don't fit into a KPI. They don't make pretty graphs. But they are everything.

You can't quantify:

- » The client who refers you without being asked, not because they're incentivized, but because they believe in you so much, they want their friends to win with you.
- » The teammate who stays calm when the servers crash, the Slack pings won't stop, and the client is melting down on Zoom like a human fire alarm.
- » The quiet trust you earn when you own a mistake before anyone even notices—no deflection, no spin, just honest accountability.
- » The goodwill that builds when you show up to their charity event, remember their kid's name, or send a handwritten note that says more than "per my last email."
- » The sense of safety you create when your team knows they can speak up, disagree, or try something bold without fear of being shut down.

None of these show up in a budget meeting.

DON'T MAKE THE MISTAKE OF BELIEVING THAT WHAT YOU CAN MEASURE IS THE ONLY THING THAT MATTERS.

But they show up everywhere else—in loyalty, retention, referrals, morale, and momentum. They show up when a client says, "You just get us." Or when a team member says, "This is the best place I've ever worked." They show up in the intangibles, and they're the difference between a business that runs and a business that thrives.

WHAT YOU TRACK REVEALS WHAT YOU ACTUALLY VALUE

Look at your current reports. What are you tracking? Hours billed? Revenue per client? Conversion rate? Cool.

Now ask yourself:
- Are we measuring follow-through?
- Are we tracking client satisfaction beyond a boilerplate survey?
- Are we noting internal wins when a team member stepped up, led with empathy, or saved the day without applause?

We live in a business world that's obsessed with optimization, but we forget that humans don't thrive in spreadsheets. They thrive in cultures that see them and in the communities they contribute to.

We're not saying ditch your numbers. Keep the dashboards. Watch the cash flow. But don't make the mistake of believing that what you can measure is the only thing that matters. Because if you only measure revenue, you'll prioritize volume over value. If you only measure speed, you'll sacrifice creativity for convenience. And if you only measure output, you'll burn out the people doing the work through unnecessary processes.

THE STUFF THAT BUILDS A REPUTATION (AND A LEGACY)

You know what makes people come back? What makes clients stay five, six, ten years deep? It's not just results. It's the way you made them feel along the way.

- When you called to say congrats on their big win, even though it had nothing to do with your scope.
- When you gave them honest advice that cost you short-term profit but saved them long-term pain.
- When your team stayed late, not out of fear, but out of care.

That's legacy stuff. That's reputation. That's what people will remember.

INVEST WHERE IT COUNTS

At the end of the day, the best investment you can make isn't just in systems, technology, or quarterly campaigns. It's in people. In trust. In time. In tiny, unscalable moments that add up to an unshakable foundation.

Because when you start measuring what really matters—not just what's easy to track—your business becomes more than a machine. It becomes a place people want to stay. A team people want to join. A partner people want to recommend. A brand people actually believe in. And good luck putting a formula on that.

THE PRICE VS. PARTNERSHIP TRAP

Let's talk pricing.

Every business eventually faces this moment: A long-term client says, "Hey, we love working with you ... but this other company came in a bit cheaper." And then they wait to see if you'll match it. Panic sets in. The spreadsheet flashes red. Your instinct is to slash the price and beg them to stay like a desperate ex in a rom-com.

But here's the thing: **If your value can be undone by a cheaper quote, you never had a partnership.** You had a line item. And we don't do line items. We do partnerships.

> **A SPREADSHEET MIGHT TELL YOU WHO'S PROFITABLE. BUT ONLY A CONVERSATION WILL TELL YOU WHO'S WORTH IT.**

Let them chase the bargain. You keep showing up with consistency, creativity, and care. Nine times out of ten, they'll be back. And if they're not? You've cleared room for someone who values more than your rate card.

WHEN THE NUMBERS DO MATTER

Now, let's be fair, money matters. We're not writing a Valentine to unpaid labor. You should absolutely know your numbers, track your profitability, and charge what your product or service is worth.

But here's the difference: **Let the numbers inform your relationships, not define them.**

A spreadsheet might tell you who's profitable. But only a conversation will tell you who's worth it.

Some clients grow over time. Some teammates hit their stride later. Some vendors charge more because they've been saving your butt for years without a single "I told you so." That's value, even if it doesn't fit neatly in the formula. And sometimes, you stick with a client not because they're the biggest but because they believe in you. And that belief becomes the foundation for something bigger than both of you.

UPGRADE YOUR METRICS

Here's our advice: **Keep the spreadsheets. Love the spreadsheets. But don't let them run the show.** Start tracking other metrics, too, like how often you laugh on calls. How many times clients say, "We trust your judgment." How often your team comes back from a project energized instead of exhausted. How many years someone sticks with you, not because they're locked into a contract, but because they want to. Those are the numbers that matter.

Because, in the end, businesses don't grow because of perfect math. They grow because of meaningful connections.

And trust us: There's no formula for that.

BEYOND THE SCOPE: REAL ROI THAT ACTUALLY MATTERS

This is where true client loyalty is built: outside the invoice, beyond the scope, and deep in the realm of "holy sh*t, they actually care about us."

Here's a radical idea: **You can create value for your clients without sending an invoice.**

No, this doesn't mean free work. (We've been to therapy. We've healed.) It means making strategic, intentional moves that deepen the relationship, build trust, and make your client say, "Damn . . . they're different."

This kind of ROI doesn't fit neatly in a monthly report, but it sticks—in their memory, their loyalty, and their willingness to refer you to anyone who'll listen.

> # GREAT WORK GETS YOU HIRED. BUT HUMAN CONNECTION KEEPS YOU IN THE ROOM.

So, here are some billable-hour-free, ROI-rich ways to deliver value that hits harder than a "per our last email":

1) **Send the Thing They Didn't Ask For**

That updated presentation. That intro email. That competitor snapshot. That new thing you're working on that they might get value from. That "Hey, I was thinking about your company while I was having a morning coffee" moment.

Unprompted ideas = deep proof you're actually invested. Clients don't forget that sh*t.

2) Say It with a Voice Memo

Don't send a 1,000-word strategy doc. Please step away from the email. Send a two-minute voice memo. Make it personal. Casual. Clear. It's intimate. It's fast. It's human. And it will make you stand out in their inbox like a confetti cannon.

3) Remember the Small Details

Remember their kid's name. Or their launch date. Or their weird obsession with sci-fi. You're not just a vendor. You're in a relationship. Act like it.

Caring ≠ creeping. It's connection.

4) Celebrate Like a Maniac

Client hit a milestone? Closed a deal? Launched something? Celebrate like it's your win too. Send flowers or cookies. Post it. Pop a bottle on Zoom. They'll remember who clapped the loudest.

5) Make the Referral That Changes Everything

It costs you nothing. But when you say, "I know someone who could help you with that," and it actually works? You become invaluable.

Be the plug. Build the bridge. That's ROI with a heartbeat.

6) Send the Damn Handwritten Note

Yeah, yeah, it's old school. So is decency. A thirty-second scribble can earn you five years of loyalty. They'll remember it. (And probably keep it in a drawer like emotional currency.)

7) Give Them a Little Extra Armor

Clients deal with chaos too. When you prepare them for what's coming, strategically or emotionally, they trust you more.

Think: *Hey, your competitor is ramping up a new division. Just FYI.* Or: *You're about to hit a slow season. Let's prep now.* No one else is giving them foresight. Be the one who does.

8) **Be Their Thought Partner, Not Their Task Doer**

Don't just execute, engage. Ask better questions. Push back when needed. Suggest when it's silent. Be the brain, not just the button pusher.

That's ROI money can't buy.

9) **Show Up When It's Not About You**

Go to the launch party. Comment on their post. Show up at the event you weren't paid to attend. Being present without being paid = loyalty on steroids.

10) **Give a Sh*t, Genuinely**

This one's last because it's first.

If you actually give a damn about their goals, their stress, their wins, and their growth, it comes through in everything. And the ROI? That's when clients stop thinking of you as "just a vendor" and start calling you "our people."

BOTTOM LINE

Great work gets you hired. But human connection keeps you in the room.

You're not just here to deliver deliverables. You're here to create meaningful, lasting value that lives way beyond the scope doc. So, do the work, yes. But don't miss the moments that actually make it matter. Because real ROI isn't always calculated. Sometimes, it's just felt.

RULE 3

BUDGETS DON'T DEFINE BRILLIANCE

BECAUSE SOMETIMES A $5K CLIENT INSPIRES $50K WORTH OF HEART

Let's go ahead and say the thing out loud: Yes, budgets matter.

They set expectations. They frame scope. They tell us whether we're working with filet mignon or canned beans.

But here's the myth we're about to break: **A big budget doesn't always mean a valuable client. And a small budget doesn't mean small impact.**

Because, at the end of the day, money is a number. Value is a feeling.

And if you've been in business long enough, you've seen it play out: a "dream budget" with a nightmare client . . . or a shoestring project that lit your entire being on fire.

BUDGET ≠ BRILLIANCE

We've all done it.

You see the number in the proposal. It's juicy. Thick. Multiple commas. You nod like a stockbroker in a movie. You pour a fancy cup of coffee and say, "This one's going to be big."

And then three weeks later, you're in a circular hell, having an existential crisis over a client's insistence that you can do better. You've burned through the hours, the team is in a group therapy text thread, and you're no longer sure what the word "strategy" even means.

But hey, they paid well!

Now compare that to the passion project with a modest budget, the one where the client actually listened, trusted your vision, and said things like, "Wow, I never would've thought of that," instead of "Can we explore ten more versions even though I like this one?"

You gave it your all, not because the numbers were big, but because the connection was.

You wanted to go the extra mile. You wanted to surprise them. You wanted to push the boundaries because it reminded you of why you do this work in the first place.

That's the difference.

Budget buys hours. Belief buys heart.

GREAT IDEAS DON'T READ A P&L STATEMENT

Creativity is a strange beast. It doesn't matter if you're a Picasso or just average at drawing stick figures. Everyone has it in some iteration. It's not about art. It's about ideas.

It doesn't respond to money the way spreadsheets do. You can't pay it to perform. You have to inspire it. Challenge it. Feed it. Let it off the leash sometimes just to see where it runs. And while budget helps—access to tools, time, and talent—it's not the whole game.

Some of the best work we've ever done didn't come from a blank check. It came from constraints. Limitations. A deadline we weren't sure we could hit. A client who said, "We don't have much, but we believe in what this could be."

And let's be honest. Sometimes, those projects are the ones that wind up in your pitch deck, on your website, or winning you the new business. Because they weren't just about revenue.

They were about resonance.

We've seen creativity rise from the ashes of "we can't afford that." We've seen it bloom in the middle of chaos, when someone throws out a ridiculous idea that shouldn't work and suddenly does. We've watched a budding team member take a low-budget campaign and turn it into something that made everyone on the team stop and say, "Wait . . . did we just make something great?"

Why? Because when money isn't the main driver, meaning has a chance to step in.

When the pressure to "justify the budget" is off the table, people start experimenting. When there's no twenty-person client committee waiting to approve every piece, your creativity feels free to take risks. And when the expectations are low, but the belief is high, magic happens.

Let's be real. Some of the most soulless work we've done came from the highest-paid contracts. The stuff where every idea had to pass through five departments and a legal review before anyone could say, "Yeah, go for it." Where the creative brief had footnotes. Where the guidelines were less "guide" and more "maximum-security prison."

But those small, scrappy projects with big heart?

Those are the ones where creative ideas get to breathe. Where it shows up in sweatshirts, not suits. Where it says, "I don't have all the answers, but I've got a gut feeling and a weird idea. Want to try it?"

You can't manufacture that. You can't invoice for it. And you sure as hell can't plan for it in Q2.

BIG BUDGETS CAN SOMETIMES SMOTHER BIG IDEAS

Here's an inconvenient truth: **Sometimes, the more money involved, the less freedom you actually get.** Why? Because money makes people nervous. It invites more stakeholders. More opinions. More approval chains.

Suddenly, you're constrained by consensus, watering down brilliance in the name of "alignment." It's like trying to write a love song with an accounting department watching over your shoulder.

Now, we're not saying big budgets are bad. We love a good, healthy budget. We're huge fans of well-funded ideas. But the budget should be a support system, not a leash. When it becomes a muzzle, everyone loses.

THE PROJECTS YOU REMEMBER

Here's a question: When you think about the work that defined you—the stuff that made you proud, that pushed you, that made your heart race a little—how many of those projects were the highest-paying ones?

For most of us, the answer is "not many."

You remember the work that meant something. The projects where the client took a chance. Where the idea came out of nowhere, and it worked. Where the budget didn't matter because the mission did. Those are the projects that show up in your highlight reel. They remind you why you got into this wild, wonderful world of business in the first place.

CHASE THE SPARK, NOT JUST THE SPEND

So, yes, we charge what we're worth. Yes, we love a healthy scope of work. But we never, ever let budget define how much heart or the big ideas we bring to the table. Because ideas don't punch a timecard. They don't care about margins. They don't show up because the invoice cleared. They show up because something inside said, "Let's make something that matters."

So, next time you're tempted to rank a project's worth by the budget column, ask yourself this: *Does it light us up? Does it challenge us? Does it give us room to stretch, risk, and grow?*

Because if the answer's yes, then you've got value. The kind that never fits on a spreadsheet.

CLIENTS AREN'T ALL CREATED EQUAL

Not all clients are the same. You already know this. Some view you as a vendor. Others view you as a partner. Some want a product. Others want a process. Some want a transactional line item they can mark "complete." Others want a co-creator to help build something that lasts.

And while we're at it, let's drop another truth bomb: **The dollar amount a client brings in does not determine how much respect they deserve or how much effort you should give them.**

Yes, we have to be practical. Yes, bigger budgets often come with bigger teams, more pressure, and more complex deliverables. But never let size alone dictate energy.

Because there are $5,000 clients who show more appreciation, gratitude, and vision than $500,000 clients who act like they bought stock in your soul.

If you've been there, you know exactly what I mean.

FEEDING THE SOUL (AND THE SPREADSHEET)

Let's talk about soul projects.

These are the ones where something just clicks with the work, the people, the mission. They may not be paying top dollar, but they're paying attention. They let you stretch your ideas. They see the layers in what you create. They say thank you. They notice the little things.

And those projects? They feed your team in ways no invoice can. They remind people why they chose this career path instead of something less chaotic (like, say, alligator wrestling). They reignite energy. They become the spark that fuels everything else.

So, yeah, take the big-budget gigs. Do great work. Cash the checks. But never forget to make room for the work that makes your people proud.

DEFINE VALUE FOR YOURSELF

At the end of the day, value isn't determined by line items or billing rates. It's determined by what a project brings to your business, your team, and your sense of purpose.

So, here's our take:
- » Chase the client who wants to build something with you, not just through you.
- » Don't let numbers alone decide what gets your best thoughts.
- » Trust your gut when it tells you a small project has big potential.
- » And never forget: **Your time is worth more than their budget. But your joy is worth more than both.**

Because when the spreadsheets are done, and the invoices are paid, the thing you'll remember isn't the project that "made" the most. It's the one that made you "feel" the most.

FROM CREATIVE ENERGY TO HUMAN CONNECTION

So, we've established that budgets don't define value. That, sometimes, the smallest projects carry the biggest emotional weight. That creativity can't be summoned by spreadsheets or price tags.

But here's where it all clicks into place: **Even the best, boldest, most brilliant work means nothing without the relationship behind it.**

Your work might wow someone. But it's your character, your trust, your humanity that makes them want to come back. Again and again.

And when you zoom out—beyond the pitch decks and pretty pixels—the pattern becomes clear: **Our greatest successes have never come just from the work. They've come from the people who believed in it. And more importantly, the people who believed in us.**

RULE 4

PEOPLE DO BUSINESS WITH PEOPLE

YOUR BEAUTIFUL WORK WON'T SAVE YOU FROM BEING A JERK

Let me take you back.
I was in my twenties. Hungry. Scrappy. Deep in the game of building what I thought would be a legendary creative career. I had just finished a rebrand that I believed was going to change everything and maybe even land me on the cover of some industry magazine or at least get a standing ovation at a pitch meeting.

The execution? Flawless. The strategy? Tight. The visual identity? A masterpiece. I was so proud I practically wanted to frame the presentation and hang it in my bathroom where I could admire it daily.

Then, I showed it to a mentor, someone who had been in business since people were faxing contracts and storing client data in filing cabinets. He looked at it, smiled, and said:

"It's good. But people don't do business with art. They do business with people. Be human first. Be creative second. Show them you understand them."

Excuse me? Sir, did you miss the brilliance of slide 17?

But he wasn't wrong. And that little gut punch stuck with me. Because it's not just about your work or the end product. It's about the way you treat people along the way. That's what gets remembered. That's what gets referred. That's what builds businesses that last longer than your latest highlight reel.

PEOPLE HIRE ENERGY—NOT JUST OUTCOMES

It doesn't matter if you're building a brand, a product, a consulting empire, or a local coffee shop. Your work might be world-class. Your deliverables might be tight. Your strategy could walk itself into a boardroom. But if people hate working with you? It's game over.

The relationship is the result.

People hire those they like. They refer those they trust. They stay loyal to those who show up. Not the ones who flex expertise and leave them feeling dumb. Not the ones who talk in circles to avoid accountability. Not the ones who nickel-and-dime every change request like they're billing by the comma.

THE WORK DOESN'T CARRY THE RELATIONSHIP—YOU DO

Want to know a dirty little secret? Most clients don't remember your best work. They don't think about your spreadsheets late at night. They don't tuck your products or service under their pillow and dream of synergy.

They remember that you picked up the phone when they were panicking. That you didn't sigh when they asked their third dumb question. That you laughed at the right time. That you made them feel like they were more than just a line item on your invoice.

> **WHEN YOU MISS THE HUMAN ELEMENT, EVEN GREAT WORK CAN FEEL FLAT.**

That's the glue. That's the sticky stuff. And if you want long-term partnerships, not just one-night-stand projects, you've got to lead with that energy.

We've all had clients we crushed it for, and the work was amazing, but the relationship fizzled. Why? Because we were focused on output, not connection. We forgot that while we were obsessing over the details internally, they were obsessing over a board meeting they were dreading.

We treated the project like a work exercise. They were treating it like a career move.

When you miss the human element, even great work can feel flat.

Now flip it. Think of your longest-standing, most loyal clients. The ones who keep coming back. The ones who refer you like it's their side hustle. Are they sticking around because your last email had excellent visual hierarchy? Or are they sticking around because they like working with you and all your typos?

Exactly.

The longer I've been in this game, the more I realize the real competitive advantage isn't what's in your portfolio. It's what's in your personality.

THE HUMAN ROI: TRUST, HUMOR, AND THE "I GOT YOU" FACTOR

Let's break it down. Here's what clients actually value … the stuff that doesn't show up in a portfolio but keeps the engine running:

- » **Trust:** They believe you'll do what you say you'll do. Every time. No weird surprises. No smoke and mirrors. Just solid, honest work.
- » **Responsiveness:** You respond. You don't ghost. You make them feel like a priority, not a slot on a task list.

- » **Humor:** Seriously. Humor goes a long way. Clients are stressed. If you can make them laugh during a rough week, you're halfway to a lifetime relationship.
- » **The "I got you" energy:** You've got their back. You think ahead. You anticipate problems before they show up on their radar. You're the calm in their chaos.

That's the stuff that makes you indispensable. So, let's talk about it.

THE "I GOT YOU" ENERGY

This right here? This is the magic.

Forget fancy marketing, slick talking points, and over-rehearsed industry jargon. If you want to build trust, loyalty, and long-term partnerships, what clients really want, and what they're quietly praying for, is someone who gives off "I got you" energy.

What does that mean?

It means you're the steady hand on the wheel when the road gets bumpy. You anticipate the speed bumps. You pack the snacks. You make sure the tires are rotated and the playlist is right. You're not just there for the ride; you're driving with confidence and foresight. You're the one who says, "Don't worry. We saw this coming. Here's what we're going to do."

And suddenly, their blood pressure drops.

What They Actually Want (But Won't Put in the RFP)

Here's the stuff no client will ever write down in a brief, but is secretly at the top of their wish list:

- » **Clarity over confusion.** Don't make them guess what you're saying.
- » **Consistency over charisma.** Being a rock beats being a genius.
- » **Humor over hustle porn.** Make them laugh. They'll call you first every time.

- » **Empathy over ego.** Listen. Ask. Care. It works in every industry.
- » **Responsiveness over perfection.** Reply first. Polish later.

People are drowning in stress. They don't just want the job done; they want someone who makes them feel safer, smarter, more capable. They're not looking for superheroes. They're looking for humans who make their job easier.

You Think Ahead

"I got you" means you're already five steps ahead. You've read the brief, but you're also reading between the lines.

- » You catch the potential snag in their timeline before it becomes a fire drill.
- » You notice that the board meeting is coming up, and you bump up your deadline without being asked because you know how they like to walk into big meetings prepared.
- » You flag an inconsistency before anyone on their team does.
- » You remind them that their new product launch is over a holiday weekend and kindly steer them back to reality.

You're not just delivering on what was asked. You're delivering on what wasn't but should have been.

You Solve Problems Quietly

Some people show off their work by making sure everyone sees the fire they put out.

"I got you" energy doesn't need applause.

It's humble. It's quiet. It's behind the scenes, orchestrating calm in the middle of client chaos like some kind of well-caffeinated Gandalf.

You fix things without fanfare. You smooth things out before they wrinkle. You're not dramatic about it. You're just reliable. And that reliability is rare, which makes it incredibly valuable.

Because when you have "I got you" energy, your clients start sleeping better. They stop micromanaging. They trust. They focus on their world because they know you're handling yours.

You Stay Calm When They Spiral

Clients are human. They panic. They overreact. They forget everything you told them last week and send a 17-paragraph email that ends with "We're just really concerned...."

That's your cue.

"I got you" energy is not reactive. It doesn't match chaos with chaos. It shows up steady, confident, and in control.

You reply with clarity. You strip the drama from the moment. You show them a path through the fog. You might even crack a light joke just to take the edge off because, sometimes, people just need to feel okay again.

And here's the best part: **That calm becomes addictive.**

Clients will start looping you in on things outside your scope because they trust your instincts. You become their steady, their compass, their secret weapon.

You Protect Their Reputation Like It's Your Own

"I got you" doesn't just mean you're good at your job. It means you're protecting them and their reputation, their time, their energy.

You write emails that they can forward to their team without editing. You craft messages that make them look like geniuses. You build strategies that make them say, "This is exactly what I needed."

They'll stick with you not because you always get it right—but because you never leave them hanging.

You Become the Person They Call First

"I got you" energy makes you the first call when everything goes right and the only call when everything goes wrong.

It's not about perfection. It's about presence.

It's about being dependable in a world where too many people flake, bail, or blame.

It's about doing great work and being the kind of person who never lets someone feel alone in the chaos.

Give your clients that consistently, and they'll never forget it. Because when the world gets loud, stressful, and unpredictable, you become the calm in the storm.

You become the person they trust.

And trust, more than any product, strategy, or new idea, is the most valuable deliverable you'll ever produce.

REPUTATION IS BUILT IN THE MOMENTS NO ONE SEES

You want to build a reputation that lasts? Don't just be good in the pitch meeting. Be good in the awkward follow-up call. Be kind when they miss their deadline. Be understanding when they change direction for the fifth time.

Those are the moments that define you. That's what gets remembered when they grow their business or move to a new company and suddenly need a trusted partner. That's what gets you recommended at dinner tables and in their emails to colleagues you didn't know existed.

Be the person who leaves a trail of "They were incredible to work with" in your wake. That kind of brand equity doesn't need an ad campaign. It spreads by word of mouth, by energy, by the way you make people feel.

YOUR WORK GETS YOU IN THE DOOR. YOUR CHARACTER GETS YOU THE KEYS.

When you do great work, people notice. It's your invitation to the table. But if you want to stay at that table? You better bring good people skills and a decent sense of humor.

In business, people don't hire products or portfolios. They hire people they trust to make them look smart, calm, and capable when things hit the fan. They hire people who listen, who solve, who don't make them feel like an idiot for not knowing what your industry terms mean. And if you can do all that while delivering great work? Well, now you've got a client for life, not just for the quarter.

TRUST IS YOUR REAL DELIVERABLE

Anyone can build a funnel, run the numbers, or write a proposal. But when you create a relationship that runs on trust? You're not just solving a business problem. You're becoming part of the business itself. And when your clients start texting you outside the project scope, inviting you to strategy meetings, or saying, "We trust your gut on this one," you've leveled up. You're not a vendor anymore. You're the steady hand. The advisor. The friend who can speak the hard truths and still get invited back to the next meeting.

PEOPLE DON'T DO BUSINESS WITH DELIVERABLES. THEY DO BUSINESS WITH PEOPLE THEY TRUST TO GIVE A DAMN.

That's the power of you. The human part. The part that can't be duplicated, templated, or replaced by AI.

HERE'S YOUR NEW RULE:

People don't do business with deliverables. They do business with people they trust to give a damn. So, don't just show up with tools and talent. Show up with tact. With timing. With empathy. With humor. With presence. With that steady "I got you" vibe that makes people say, "Damn... I don't just want to work with them again. I want them in the room every time."

Make the work great. But make the relationship unforgettable. That's the kind of ROI you can't measure, but everyone remembers.

RULE 5

PASSION > PERFECTION

BECAUSE PERFECT IS BORING
AND PASSION PAYS DIVIDENDS

PASSION > PERFECTION

L et's go ahead and say it: **Perfection is a lie made up by insecure overachievers.**

You don't need it. Your clients don't want it. And spoiler alert: **No one notices it.**

What people DO notice? Passion. Energy. Creative obsession. That spark in your eye when you talk about the idea you just can't let go of, even though it wasn't in the original scope, isn't technically billable, and may or may not involve googling "how to shoot a flaming logo without burning down your garage."

That's the stuff that moves people. That's the stuff that sells. That's what people want to hire and be around.

So, let's stop chasing perfection like it's the holy grail. It's not the goal. Passion is. Passion gets sh*t done. Passion takes risks. Passion changes the room.

PERFECTION IS POLISHED. PASSION IS MAGNETIC.

Perfection shows up in pressed slacks with a printed agenda. Passion shows up slightly late but brimming with ideas and holding a coffee that's probably not theirs.

One wants to look good. The other wants to make something great. Guess which one actually creates momentum?

We've hired both types. We've worked with both types. And we can tell you with absolute certainty: **We'll take passionate chaos over polished blandness every time.** Because passionate people give a damn. They care. Sometimes, too much. They'll send texts at midnight with wild ideas that actually aren't bad. They'll fight for things that matter and maybe get a little too attached to things—but you know what? You'll never have to wonder if they're engaged.

FIREWORKS OR FIREWOOD?

Let's talk about real passion.

Real passion isn't always loud. It doesn't need a sign or a LinkedIn banner to prove it's working. Passion doesn't show up in a blazer and a presentation voice. Some people just have it in their blood, and some people just want you to think they do. You can usually tell the difference pretty fast. One is fireworks. The other is firewood.

> # PERFECTION MIGHT IMPRESS A ROOM. BUT PASSION? PASSION WARMS THE WHOLE DAMN BUILDING.

Fireworks are flashy.

They show up like caffeinated cheerleaders. They sparkle, crackle, and light up the whole room. They come in hot. Big energy. Loud opinions. Big drama and big "look at me!" vibes.

They blow up on day one, steal the spotlight, and leave a cloud of smoke behind them by lunch. They're exciting as hell... for a moment.

But give it time, and they're gone. Burnt out. Moved on. No heat. No staying power. Just noise and ashes. And you (or someone else) has to clean up their mess—in the break room and the boardroom.

Firewood, though? It's a different kind of magic.

It takes a little time to catch. You've got to stack it right. Feed it a little air. But when it lights? It burns. Long, steady, and strong. It warms the room, cooks the food, and fuels the whole place. You don't have to babysit it. You just have to respect it. And it lasts... long after the fireworks crowd has ghosted the group.

This is how you spot the people who are built to last. They're not always the first to speak up in meetings. They don't need the spotlight. But give them a problem that matters and a match, and watch what they build.

Don't hire for hype. Hire for heat. Don't chase the excitement. Chase the energy. Hire the burn. Not the bang. Because perfection might impress a room. But passion? Passion warms the whole damn building.

PASSION ISN'T ALWAYS LOUD—BUT IT'S ALWAYS PRESENT

Let's not confuse passion with volume.

Some of the most passionate people we know are quiet. Intentional. Introspective. They don't jump on tables, but their work punches you in the gut. Their ideas come from deep wells. They care so much it hurts sometimes.

You don't have to be wild to be passionate. You just have to care deeply. Passion isn't a personality trait. It's a fuel source.

So, don't go looking for loud. Look for people who give a damn. People who bring heart into meetings, the ones who want to do work that means something. Those people don't need to be managed. They need to be empowered.

PASSIONATE PEOPLE ARE CHALLENGING

Let's address the uncomfortable truth: **Passionate people are not easy.**

They ask questions. They push boundaries. They don't always "stay in their lane" because they're too busy caring about the whole car. They have strong opinions about color psychology and Slack etiquette. They want to change things. And they want to do it yesterday. And yeah, sometimes, they make meetings longer. But they also make ideas better.

Perfection seeks harmony. Passion seeks impact.

If you want a team of nodding heads and quiet compliance, by all means, hire for perfection. But if you want people who will make your business more interesting, creative, and full of actual momentum? Hire passion.

Then, lead them. Coach them. Channel that intensity into something useful. Because once you learn how to harness passion to refine it, not mute it, you'll stop spending your time motivating people and start partnering with fire.

WANT IT VS. WANT TO WANT IT

There's a difference, and it matters more than you think.

We all say we WANT IT. The business. The success. The executive life. The control. The freedom. The big vision on the wall and the bank account to match.

But some people really want it—like lose sleep, chase ideas, stay uncomfortable, push limits kind of want it.

And then there are people who WANT to want it.

They like the idea of the hustle. They love watching others chase dreams. They post the quotes, buy the planners, download the courses... but when it comes time to bleed for it? To show up early, stay late, fail fast, and take feedback without falling apart?

They fizzle.

Not because they're bad. But because they're in love with the image, not the process. They forsake the time of planting and watering. All the time it takes to put in the work. They just want the reward of the harvest.

But the Real Ones? They're addicted to momentum. They can't not work the problem. They're allergic to stagnation. They're curious, annoying, relentless, annoying again, and then brilliant. They don't need the stage. They live for the solution.

So, how do you tell the difference?

Want-It People:

» **Ask better questions.** Not "What's my deadline?" but "How can this be better?"
» **Don't wait to be told.** They move first, ask second, and figure it out in motion.
» **Get louder when stakes go up.** They lean in when the room gets quiet. Chaos turns them on.
» **Feel like a wind at your back.** They make you better without trying. Their momentum is contagious.
» **Apologize when they mess up, not when they speak up.** Confidence isn't ego. It's ownership.
» **Run out of hours before they run out of ideas.** They want the work to breathe. They care if it sings.

Want-to-Want-It People:

» **Obsess over optics.** They care more about looking "busy" than being productive.
» **Start strong, fade fast.** Give them a new idea, and they're all in . . . until it requires actual work.
» **Need to be nudged. Constantly.** You'll feel like a motivational speaker instead of a collaborator.

- » **Ask questions they already know the answer to.** Because they want to sound engaged—but not risk getting it wrong.
- » **Avoid the hard parts.** Feedback? Conflict? Late nights? Suddenly, you can't find them anywhere.
- » **Show up when it's fun. Disappear when it's not.** Passion that depends on conditions isn't passion; it's performance.

THE GIFTS VS. LEPROSY TEST

Let me tell you a story.

We had a team member once. A brilliant guy. Charismatic. Creative as hell. The kind of person who "wowed" us with his work. Someone who could walk into a room and have everyone eating out of his hand before he even opened his laptop. He was a friend too. One of those people you root for—hard. And that's what made it tough.

He had all the ingredients: skill, vision, charm, instincts. I used to joke that he could own the damn world if he ever just learned to hold his fire, to rein in the impulsive, undisciplined parts long enough to let his talent win. But here's the thing: **Likable and teachable are not the same thing.**

The people who Want It? They're hungry. But more importantly, they're coachable. They're willing to adjust. To learn. To fall on their sword if it means getting better. Their passion isn't just flashy; it's sustainable, because it adapts.

The people who Want to Want It? They flash. They spark. They have "moments" that make you believe in them again, right before they vanish back into inconsistency, excuses, or emotional volatility. Their passion comes with a ticking clock. And eventually, you start noticing something else: the pattern.

I had a mentor tell me once to always ask this question when evaluating someone's performance, character, or potential: Is this an incident or a pattern? Everyone screws up. Everyone has bad days.

Everyone needs a course correction now and then. That's human. That's forgivable. That's an incident. But when it happens again. And again. And again. That's no longer a bad day. That's a track record. A pattern worth paying attention to. And that's a problem.

AT SOME POINT, THE BRILLIANCE DOESN'T MATTER IF THE BEHAVIOR IS CORROSIVE.

This teammate? Over time, the missteps became consistent. The drama, the missed cues, the emotional wear-and-tear on the team ... it wasn't a bad stretch anymore. It was a pattern. And it came with something else I've never forgotten: **leprosy**.

Now stay with me.

Leprosy, metaphorically speaking, is the stuff in someone's character that's just hard to look past. The unsightly, self-sabotaging parts that keep showing up. We all have it. None of us is flawless. But leprosy left untreated, ignored, or unacknowledged starts to spread. Starts to infect. Starts to stink up the room in a way that not even talent can mask.

At some point, the brilliance doesn't matter if the behavior is corrosive. The "potential" doesn't outweigh the pattern. Their leprosy stops affecting just them and starts affecting everyone. And here's the really tough pill: **If you're not careful, you'll start exhibiting symptoms.**

So, we had to make the hard call. We let him go. Not because he wasn't gifted. Not because we didn't care. But because passion without accountability is just a fire hazard.

You can be the most talented person in the room, but if no one wants to stand next to you when the heat gets turned up, you're not leadership material. You're a liability with a good-looking résumé.

Wanting it means showing up even when it's uncomfortable. It means being coachable, not just charismatic. It means treating your "leprosy" before it infects the culture around you. Because a person's gifts and talents can open the door. But leprosy will clear the room.

Here's the part no one likes to talk about: **Sometimes, *you're* the one who Wants to Want It.**

Yep. All of us have been there. The seasons when we're tired. The burnout. The drifting. The *Why does it even matter?* spirals. It's okay. The point isn't shame; it's self-awareness. The goal isn't perfection. The goal is awareness. And the second you recognize you've started pretending to care more than you do, that's the moment you can get real, reset, and reignite.

When you feel yourself slipping into "want-to-want-it" mode, it's your cue. Check your inputs. Revisit your "why." Light the damn fire again. No one else can do it for you.

Because passion isn't just nice to have. It's a radar. A compass. A signal. And when it fades, everything else starts to flicker too.

Whether you're leading a team, hiring for a role, or looking in the mirror, ask yourself: *Is this still lighting me up? Or am I just doing what looks lit? Do they (or I) really want this—or just want to want it?* One burns bright. The other burns out.

Choose wisely.

WHEN PASSION AND PERFECTION START TO BRAWL

Let's be honest: **Passion and perfection can both be loud as hell.**

One yells, "Let's build something!" The other whispers, "But it better be flawless, or don't even bother." They're both convincing. They both sound like drive. But only one of them actually finishes anything. Because while passion moves things forward, perfectionism is the handbrake disguised as quality control.

"DONE" IS A MOVING TARGET WHEN PERFECTION IS DRIVING.

It looks noble. It sounds professional. But too often, it's just fear that's all dressed up.

THE TRUTH ABOUT THE TUG-OF-WAR

I've started projects and never finished them because the version in my head was cleaner than the mess I felt I was making.

Wait. Go read that again.

I've delayed amazing ideas, postponed killer drafts, and second-guessed potential brilliance because it just never felt DONE. But "done" is a moving target when perfection is driving.

And passion? Passion doesn't care about polish. It cares about impact. That's the fight, and every person knows it. Passion wants to ignite. Perfection wants to edit. And if you're not careful, perfection will castrate your momentum.

PERFECTION IS THE KILLER OF MOVEMENT

We say we're "revising." We say we're "tweaking." We say we're "waiting until it's ready."

But if we're honest, most of the time, we're just afraid.
- » Afraid it won't be as good as it is in our head.
- » Afraid people won't get it.
- » Afraid it won't land.
- » Afraid it'll prove we're not as good as we hope we are.

But here's the truth: **You can't test an idea that never ships.** You can't impact anyone with a draft still sitting in your Google Drive.

THE BALANCE: BUILD, THEN POLISH

Let passion drive the first draft. Let it be messy. Unhinged. Full of feeling. Let it live before you kill it with edits. Then, once the thing exists, invite your perfectionist brain in to clean it up. But never, and I mean never, let perfection go first. Because if it does, your work dies at the gate.

Confession: **This book is a product of the never-ending edit.** I've always written out my thoughts as they come to me. Messages and scribbles I had made over the last twenty years or so. Jotting down notes here and there. Small things I've learned. Collecting and polishing some over the years. And that's where they sat—in my drafts folder. I propped them up on my mantle of misfortune. And I never let all that stuff get past the refining floor . . . until now.

Better late than never! Isn't that what good little perfectionists say?

PASSION BUILDS. PERFECTION REFINES.

Passion is the fire. Perfection is the furnace. One gives it energy. The other shapes it.

But if you start with the furnace, you'll never light the match. And if you only live in the fire, nothing ever gets finished. You need both. But they have to come in the right order.

YOUR WORK DOESN'T NEED TO BE PERFECT. IT NEEDS TO LIVE.

So, next time you feel stuck—not blocked, not busy, just frozen—ask yourself: *Is this moment fueled by passion? Or is perfection driving the wheel again?* If it's passion, keep going. If it's perfection, take the wheel back.

Your work doesn't need to be perfect. It needs to live.

FINAL THOUGHT: PROGRESS > PERFECTION. PASSION > ALL.

Perfect is a myth. It's a moving target. And spoiler alert: **Most "perfect" things are overthought, underwhelming, and completely forgettable.**

But passionate work? That's the stuff that lives. That breathes. That explodes with energy and imperfection and life.

So, here's the rule: **Hire for passion**. Work with people who are on fire for what they do.

Lead with energy. Let go of "flawless" and embrace the flawed-but-inspired. And if you're feeling stuck? Reignite your own damn passion. Because the minute you do? The universe starts paying attention.

RULE 6

DEI—DO EVERYTHING INTENTIONALLY

BECAUSE "WINGING IT" IS NOT A SCALABLE BUSINESS STRATEGY

DEI—DO EVERYTHING INTENTIONALLY

Let's be clear: **This ain't your corporate DEI training.**
No slides. No icebreakers. No one's making you pretend to be a tree.

In this chapter, DEI stands for "Do Everything Intentionally." And if that sounds exhausting, congratulations, you've officially been overbooked, overcaffeinated, and under-inspired for too long.

Doing everything intentionally doesn't mean lighting sage before every meeting or journaling about your mission statement during lunch breaks. It just means: stop doing sh*t on autopilot.

YOU CAN TEACH SKILLS. YOU CANNOT TEACH SOMEONE TO GIVE A DAMN.

Stop defaulting to "because we've always done it that way." Stop hiring warm bodies and hoping they figure it out. Stop saying yes to projects that make your stomach hurt before the kickoff call.

You want a business that works? Build it on purpose. Not out of panic.

YOUR TEAM SHOULDN'T BE AN ACCIDENTAL GROUP CHAT

Let's talk about hiring. Or, as many businesses call it: "Just grab someone who can kind of do the thing." That's how you end up with Susan, who's great at spreadsheets but kills the vibe in every meeting like a tax audit.

Here's the thing: **You're not just hiring skillsets. You're hiring energy.** You're hiring someone's attitude, instincts, sense of ownership, and whether or not they're going to break Slack with inspirational memes or passive-aggressive emoji replies.

We don't want the guy who can "do the job." We want the one who wants the job. Who wants the challenge. Who walks in thinking, *Let me make this better, faster, or at least 17 percent cooler.*

You can teach skills. You cannot teach someone to give a damn.

And while we're here . . . "culture fit" isn't code for "someone I'd get a beer with." It's "Does this person care about the things we care about? Will they show up like this work actually means something?"

Hire people who move with purpose, not just polish.

INTENTION IN → BULLSH*T OUT

Let's flip the camera around: If you keep attracting clients with chaotic energy, terrible communication habits, and the emotional intelligence of a parking meter, guess what?

You might be part of the problem.

Ask yourself:

» Are you putting out intentional messaging about how you work and what you value?
» Are you setting expectations with confidence, or rolling over like a golden retriever in a thunderstorm?

» Are you leading your company, or are you letting "anyone with a budget" lead you?

The clients you attract are often a reflection of your clarity (or lack thereof).

If you put out desperation, you'll attract drama. If you put out "please like us," you'll get ghosted. But if you lead with conviction, clarity, and confidence, guess what shows up?

People who move like you move. People who respect your process. People who trust your judgment. People who don't send 3 a.m. emails that start with "Quick thought..."

You attract what you reflect.

So, if your calendar looks like a circus and your inbox feels like a hostage situation, it might be time to check what energy you're leaking into the universe.

DO EVERYTHING LIKE IT MATTERS (BECAUSE IT DOES)

Here's the most dangerous lie in business: "This part doesn't matter. Just get it done." That's how cultures erode. That's how talent walks out. That's how trust evaporates: one careless Slack message, one ignored idea, one "meh" deliverable at a time.

Doing everything intentionally doesn't mean obsessing over every process and micromanaging your team's keyboard shortcuts.

It means showing up with a clear why:
» Why this project matters.
» Why this person was hired.
» Why you said yes to this client.
» Why you're putting this kind of energy into the work.

When intention is missing, effort becomes performative. But when intention is present? Every decision becomes a statement. Every action becomes a signal of what kind of business you run and what kind of people you want in it.

DON'T BUILD A BUSINESS YOU WANT TO ESCAPE FROM

Here's a spicy thought: **If you're daydreaming about quitting your business to become a barista in the Blue Ridge Mountains or launch a candle brand called "FML & Co."—that's a red flag.**

> **BUILD EVERYTHING AROUND YOUR ACTUAL LIFE. DON'T REVERSE-ENGINEER YOUR CALENDAR AROUND YOUR CLIENTS.**

We glamorize the grind. Celebrate being "booked and busy." Romanticize 2 a.m. edits and inbox zero. And then wake up wondering why we're fantasizing about disappearing into the woods with no Wi-Fi and a flip phone.

That's not entrepreneurship. It's actually more like escape artistry.

You didn't leave your job to create a life of freedom just to accidentally build a prison with Slack notifications. And yet, here we are.

Build everything around your actual life. Don't reverse-engineer your calendar around your clients. Reverse-engineer your business around your energy, needs, and the version of yourself you want to be awake with every day.

If your business doesn't fit your actual life, you will resent it. And when resentment builds, ideas die, and your Google Drive starts filling up with half-finished business plans for alpaca farms in Vermont.

If you're constantly dreaming of shutting it all down, maybe you don't need a new business. You just need to **run this one differently**.

So, take a deep breath. Light the "This Meeting Could've Been an Email" candle. And ask yourself the real questions: *Am I building something that gives me life? Or just something that looks good on LinkedIn while secretly stealing my soul?*

Only one of those is worth scaling.

BUILD IT ON PURPOSE OR BURN IT OUT BY ACCIDENT

So, yeah, DEI: Do Everything Intentionally. Build intentionally. Hire intentionally. Work intentionally. Communicate intentionally. Rest intentionally. (Yes, even rest. Take a damn vacation. The business will survive. And if it doesn't, congratulations, you just found a new boundary to set.)

Spoiler: **Balance Isn't Magic. It's Math.**

Because here's the real truth no one prints in the business books: You don't accidentally end up with a great business. You build it. One intentional choice at a time. If you're scaling chaos, you're not winning; you're just accelerating burnout.

So, don't wing it.

Don't wait for clarity to magically arrive.

Don't default to what's easy.

And for the love of your team, your clients, and your own sanity . . .

Do. Everything. Intentionally.

RULE 7

EVERYTHING IS AN EXPERIMENT

SPOILER: NO ONE KNOWS WHAT THE HELL THEY'RE DOING

Here's a truth no one tells you when you start a business: **Everything—and I mean everything—is an experiment.**

The pricing. The packaging. The pitch deck. The team structure. The Tuesday standups. The decision to offer kombucha in the office fridge. Every single thing you're doing? It's a giant, beautiful, sometimes-dumb experiment.

And you know what?

That's okay. That's how it's supposed to be.

Because there is no formula. There's no secret playbook. And anyone who tells you they've "cracked the code" is probably trying to sell you a course that includes ninety-seven Canva templates and a 90-minute Zoom about "funnel optimization."

The reality? Even the big guys—the billion-dollar, global, Fortune 500, "we have a TikTok team" companies—are guessing. They're experimenting, failing, pivoting, and face-planting just like the rest of us.

Let's not pretend we're above the mess. Let's embrace the mess and call it what it is: science. With branding.

THERE IS NO CHECKLIST FOR SUCCESS (SORRY)

If you're hoping for a magic checklist that guarantees success, I've got bad news and a dry-erase board full of bad decisions to show you.

There's no checklist. There's no 12-step sequence. No plug-and-play blueprint.

Why?

Because what works for one business might be a dumpster fire for another.

You are not Apple. You are not Taco Bell. You are not a legacy brand with a war chest and seventeen layers of management who all signed off on that $7 million commercial that made zero sense.

You are you. With your people. Your quirks. Your context. Your barely-holding-it-together tech stack.

So, you've got to figure out what works for you. Not what's trending on LinkedIn. Not what Gary Vee yelled about last week. You.

That's the formula: **There is no formula.**

EVERYONE SCREWS UP (EVEN THE ICONS)

Think you're too good to mess up?

Cool. So was Apple when they released the iPhone 4 with an antenna that only worked when you didn't hold the phone.

So was Coca-Cola when they tried to replace their iconic formula with "New Coke," which was basically like Pepsi with an identity crisis.

So was Taco Bell when they . . . well, they're Taco Bell. Honestly, we expect a little chaos. But still, they've had lawsuits over their meat content. Their MEAT.

These are billion-dollar companies. With departments full of experts and entire buildings full of people who have meetings about meetings.

And they still f*ck it up sometimes.

So, if you think your small business has to run flawlessly like a Swiss watch made of angel tears—relax. You're going to make mistakes. Bad hires. Dumb decisions. Overcommitments. Underdeliveries.

You're going to ship some things that are . . . not your best. That's not failure. That's data.

MAJOR COMPANIES THAT FAILED BEFORE THEY FLEW

1) **Apple**
   - The Failure: The Apple Newton. A clunky, overpriced PDA that flopped in the '90s.
   - The Win: The iPhone. They learned from the Newton failure to create the most iconic consumer tech product of all time.

2) **Netflix**
   - The Failure: Tried to sell to Blockbuster in 2000. Got laughed out of the room.
   - The Win: Became the company that buried Blockbuster and redefined entertainment.

3) **Dyson**
   - The Failure: Sir James Dyson created 5,126 failed prototypes of his vacuum cleaner.
   - The Win: Prototype 5,127 revolutionized the industry and launched a billion-dollar empire.

4) **Amazon**
   - The Failure: The Fire Phone (remember that disaster?). $170M written off in 2014.
   - The Win: Amazon Web Services (AWS), which is now the backbone of half the internet and a multi-billion-dollar revenue stream.

5) **Coca-Cola**
   - The Failure: New Coke. In 1985, they reformulated their classic drink, and America lost its mind . . . in the worst way.
   - The Win: The backlash taught them the value of brand loyalty. They brought back Classic Coke and sold even more.

6) **Twitter (X)**
   » The Failure: Started as Odeo, a podcast platform. Got crushed when Apple launched iTunes podcasting.
   » The Win: Pivoted into Twitter. Built an entire new form of real-time communication.

7) **Airbnb**
   » The Failure: Original idea? Selling cereal during the 2008 election. Yes, cereal. It flopped.
   » The Win: The cereal stunt kept them alive long enough to prove the concept of short-term rentals, which disrupted global travel forever.

8) **Spanx**
   » The Failure: Sara Blakely had zero experience in fashion or manufacturing. Rejected by every male-run hosiery mill.
   » The Win: Finally found one factory that gave her a shot. Built a billion-dollar brand from her apartment floor.

9) **Nintendo**
   » The Failure: Originally sold playing cards, then moved into everything from instant rice to vacuum cleaners. All flops.
   » The Win: Found their magic in video games, launching a global legacy with Mario and friends.

10) **Ford Motor Company**
    » The Failure: Henry Ford's first two automobile companies failed before Ford Motor Company succeeded.
    » The Win: Revolutionized transportation and modern manufacturing with the assembly line.

And these are just the ones you hear about. Imagine all the ones you haven't.

EDISON DIDN'T "FAIL" 10,000 TIMES—HE JUST HAD THAT MANY BAD IDEAS FIRST

Let's talk about Thomas Edison . . . the OG King of Invention and Experimentation.

We've heard his story in one variation or another a hundred times. He didn't invent the lightbulb overnight. In fact, he supposedly "failed" 10,000 times before finding the version that worked.

> **SUCCESS DOESN'T COME FROM PERFECTION. IT COMES FROM ITERATION. FROM TRYING STUFF. FROM EXPERIMENTING LONG ENOUGH TO FINALLY FIND OUT.**

When asked about it, Edison didn't say, "Yeah, that was humiliating, and I cried into my kerosene lamp every night."

No.

Essentially, he said, "I have not failed 10,000 times. I have not even failed once. I have succeeded in proving that those 10,000 ways will not work."

That's either an inspiring reframe or the world's most confident humblebrag. Either way, it's the truth.

Success doesn't come from perfection. It comes from iteration. From trying stuff. From experimenting long enough to finally find out.

So, what makes you think your product, email sequence, onboarding workflow, or client process needs to be perfect on the first try? It doesn't. It needs to be live. It needs to be tried and refined like an A/B-tested concept. It needs to breathe, evolve, and, yes, sometimes, fall flat on its face like a toddler learning how gravity works.

YOUR BUSINESS IS A LAB, NOT A MUSEUM

Stop treating your business like a sacred museum exhibit where everything needs to be polished, labeled, and climate-controlled. For goodness' sake, treat it like what it is: a lab.

Experiment. Try things you haven't before. Scrap things. Revise. Rethink. Rework. Rebuild.

Try a new pricing model. Test a different meeting cadence. Let your most passionate team member pitch a weird idea just to see what happens.

Delete the thing that doesn't work. Take notes. Adjust. Repeat.

Labs are messy environments, but they're the only place your breakthroughs can happen.

MISTAKES ARE ALLOWED. WHOEVER SAID THEY WEREN'T?

Seriously, who made the rule that mistakes = failure?

Was it some sad consultant in a tucked-in golf shirt? Was it your high school econ teacher with the clip-on tie? Was it TikTok influencers who haven't been inside a real office since 2006?

Mistakes aren't the enemy. They're the tuition you pay for clarity.

Some of our best decisions were born from absolute disasters:

» We lost a client? Cool. It freed up time for a better one.
» A product launch bombed? Awesome. That audience wasn't our people anyway.

» We hired a nightmare person who cried in the bathroom and rage-messaged everyone? Great. Now we know what red flags actually look like.

Every stumble is a data point. And the faster you collect them, the faster you refine your process.

FLAWS MAKE IT HUMAN. HUMAN MAKES IT WORK.

Let's talk about authenticity—not the overused marketing buzzword that gets slapped on every brand guide like a sticker on a Hydro Flask, but actual authenticity—the kind that shows up in your mess, your learning curve, and your willingness to admit you don't have it all figured out.

Here's the paradox: **People don't fall in love with perfect. They fall in love with real.** With your rough edges. With your in-progress ideas. With the way your team owns its mistakes and keeps showing up anyway.

That's why people root for small businesses. That's why they stay loyal to founders who admit when something isn't working. That's why a half-scrappy client process can still win if it's fueled by intention, effort, and honesty.

You want to build trust? Don't pretend to be polished. Be present. Be learning. Be genuine.

WHY WE STILL EAT AT CHAIN RESTAURANTS (AND IT'S NOT JUST THE FRIES)

Look, nobody goes to a Taco Bell expecting a Michelin-star experience. You go because you want something that's realistic, immediate, and maybe slightly questionable, but consistently in motion.

They try new things. Sometimes, it's genius. (Nacho fries.) Sometimes, it's a crime. (The Seafood Salad of 1986. Look it up. It happened.) But they try. They evolve. They experiment. They own their brand. And in that process, they become familiar and trusted, not because they always get it right, but because they're committed to figuring it out in real time.

People love that.

It's the same with your business. Clients don't expect you to be flawless, but they do want to know that you care, that you're adapting, and that you'll still be standing (and improving) when the cheese hits the fan.

YOUR FLAWS ARE PROOF YOU'RE EVOLVING

Flaws aren't disqualifiers. They're receipts that you're in the lab: testing, trying, growing, making progress.

You want to connect with people? Show them your version of the messed-up seafood salad. Tell them about the idea that tanked. Talk about the launch that flatlined. Share the pitch that bombed so hard your soul briefly left your body.

Not because it's cute. But because it's relatable. And because it shows that you're willing to swing, even if you miss sometimes.

IN A WORLD FULL OF CURATED BULLSH*T, THE BUSINESS THAT SAYS, "HEY, WE'RE EXPERIMENTING, BUT WE GIVE A DAMN," IS THE ONE THAT EARNS THE LOYALTY.

Authenticity doesn't come from saying, "We're authentic." It comes from doing the work, owning the misses, and letting people see the journey instead of just the highlight reel.

POLISHED IS FINE. REAL IS BETTER.

Look, you can sand the edges and pretty up the process later. But don't hide the reality of where you are. That's where the relatability lives. That's where the trust is built. That's where your voice gets its edge.

Your audience doesn't need perfect. They need to know you're in it—fully, intentionally, and unapologetically figuring it out as you go.

Be messy. Be bold. Be authentic as hell.

Because in a world full of curated bullsh*t, the business that says, "Hey, we're experimenting, but we give a damn," is the one that earns the loyalty.

EMBRACE THE CHAOS. CALL IT SCIENCE.

Your business will never be done. It will never be finished. It will never run perfectly, effortlessly, like some Instagram-friendly productivity fantasy where everyone smiles and drinks branded water out of minimalist bottles.

It will be messy. Scrappy. Flawed. Glorious. Because it's a living, breathing thing. Built by humans. Not robots. Not algorithms. Not checklists.

So, the next time something breaks? Laugh. Fix it. Write it down. Try something else. Then, pat yourself on the back and say, "It's cool. Everything's an experiment."

Because that's what it is. And that's what it'll always be.

WELCOME TO THE LAB

Here's what we know for sure: Your business isn't a perfect machine. It's not a polished presentation. It's not a clean, airtight system you set once and walk away from like a George Foreman grill.

It's a lab.

A messy, unpredictable, gloriously imperfect place where you mix things, blow some stuff up, try new ingredients, scrap the things that taste weird, and occasionally—magically—create something people fall in love with.

You're not supposed to have it all figured out. You're supposed to be trying. That's what separates people who build something meaningful from people who just build something . . . standard.

So, here's your permission slip:

- » F*ck up.
- » Try weird ideas.
- » Hire someone with no résumé but all the fire.
- » Kill the process that everyone hates.
- » Launch the thing that scares you.
- » Be honest when it doesn't work.
- » Adjust. Repeat. Keep going.

Because nothing great ever came from playing it safe in a spreadsheet. Everything great came from people who said, "Let's try this and see what happens."

So, yeah, everything is an experiment. Treat it that way. Laugh when it fails. Celebrate when it works. And never stop mixing the formula.

Because the second you stop experimenting, you stop evolving. And the second you stop evolving, your business flatlines into irrelevance right next to Blockbuster, fax machines, and that time we all thought QR codes were dead.

Stay curious. Keep testing. Keep tweaking. Keep creating your own formula.

One day, you'll look up and realize the formula you stumbled on works. And you'll have done something that's incredible.

LIVE THE DAMN EXPERIMENT

I want to talk directly to those of you who are considering something big that you want to do. Maybe some of you haven't launched your business yet and are fearful to make the leap, and can't get past it yet. Or maybe you're afraid to make the next move, launch something radical, or do what you've wanted to do for years, but fear has caused you to settle for comfort over courage.

Here's the thing nobody tells you while you're clutching your paycheck like it's a flotation device: you can study, plan, and daydream forever, but there's no formula that makes courage comfortable.

My business partner and I were there once. We had cushy six-figure executive jobs. We had titles people envied, LinkedIn profiles that looked successful, and paychecks that showed up whether we crushed it or coasted. But every day we felt the gnawing: This isn't it.

So we had a choice: sit in meetings trading our time for someone else's dream, or throw ourselves headfirst into the unknown with no safety net, no guaranteed salary, and no promises beyond our belief in ourselves.

We said f*ck it. We made the leap. It was terrifying. It was liberating. It was the beginning of everything.

Most people think they need perfect timing, a fully baked plan, or a sign from the universe. Spoiler: the universe doesn't send memos. It sends moments. Gut-checks. Opportunities that make you clench your teeth and wonder if you're crazy for even considering them.

Experiments don't happen in theory. They happen when you get your hands dirty. They happen when you trade comfort for possibility. You have to live the experiment, not spectate from the sidelines.

Because when you're observing, you're safe, but you're also stagnant. Watching others launch, risk, and grow while you analyze their mistakes doesn't move your life forward. It just makes you a well-informed bystander in your own story.

The truth? You will never feel "ready." Fear doesn't evaporate when you finally have the perfect product, service, or business plan. The only way to prove to yourself you can do it is by doing it. That's what an experiment is: trying, adjusting, risking, and learning. Not knowing what's next but having the guts to light the fuse anyway.

Our leap wasn't easy. It wasn't smooth. But it's the reason you're reading this now—because if we hadn't stepped into the experiment, we'd still be living someone else's idea of success.

So take the shot. Make the jump. Leave the comfort zone that's suffocating you. Live the damn experiment, because safety nets don't build empires.

RULE 8

ACT LIKE IT, ATTRACT LIKE IT

FORGET THE "FAKE IT TILL YOU MAKE IT" TROPE

L et's go ahead and say it: **"Fake it till you make it" is garbage advice.**
It's the business world's version of duct-taping your car together and hoping no one notices. It tells you to pretend. Perform. Smile like everything's great while your inbox is melting down, and you just googled "how to write a contract from scratch."

Now, don't get it twisted. We're not against confidence. We're not against big energy. We're not even against a little improv when you're trying to keep the ship afloat.

But faking it? That sh*t's exhausting. And unsustainable. Because eventually, faking leads to flaking—on your purpose, your people, your process, and your passion.

So, let's call this what it really is. It's not about faking anything. It's about becoming the person and the business that attracts what you want.

And yes, it's intangible. Yes, it's weirdly cosmic. But so is gravity, and we don't argue with that.

"BUILD IT, AND THEY WILL COME"? NOT EXACTLY.

Let's talk about the *Field of Dreams* lie we were all sold.

"If you build it, they will come."

Sure. Cool. Inspiring. Such a good movie.

But let's be honest. You can build the most incredible thing in the world: a beautiful brand, a revolutionary offer, or the world's first low-carb cinnamon roll empire. If your energy sucks, your attitude is off, or your vibe doesn't match your own damn mission statement, people won't come. They'll scroll right past. Because people can feel when you're just going through the motions.

You know it when you see it:
» The entrepreneur whose site says, "empowered storytelling," but whose energy says, "I hate all of this and just want to nap."
» The agency that boasts "dynamic creative work" but hasn't posted anything interesting since 2019.
» The business coach who preaches mindset but looks like they're one PowerPoint template away from giving up.

You can't just build it. You have to believe it. And then act like you believe it everywhere. That's what sends the invite to the universe.

YOU ATTRACT WHAT YOU ARE. FOR REAL.

Not what you say you are. Not what you post on your About page. Not what your thirty-second elevator pitch implies.

The energy you carry—the passion, the drive, the curiosity, the purpose, the clarity—that's what calls people in.

Think about it: **When you're lit up about your work, opportunities show up.**

When you're stuck, stressed, and cynical, somehow, your inbox fills with weird energy and "low budget, low energy" projects.

When you're clear about what you want, the right people seem to appear like it's scripted.

When you're desperate and foggy, you become a magnet for tire-kickers, time-wasters, and emotionally unavailable collaborators who say things like, "We just want to vibe it out for now." Coincidence? Nah. That's the universe mirroring your mess.

> **THE WORLD IS FULL OF TALENTED PEOPLE, BUT YOUR ENERGY IS THE GREAT ATTRACTOR THAT CAUSES THE RIGHT THINGS TO COALESCE AROUND YOU.**

This is where we get a little cosmic. Stay with me.

If you keep attracting high-maintenance clients who treat your work like a fast-food order, ask yourself: *What kind of energy am I putting out?*

If you're giving off vibes like, *We'll do whatever, just please like us*, don't be surprised when you draw in people who want to walk all over you.

But when you show up with energy, creativity, curiosity, and fire in your eyes? When you stand for something? When you love what you do and talk about it like a preacher at a tent revival? The universe (yes, the actual freaking universe) starts sending those people to your doorstep.

You attract people who vibe with you. People who respect you. Collaborators who match your intensity. Not because of luck, but because your signal is strong.

The world is full of talented people, but your energy is the great attractor that causes the right things to coalesce around you. So, don't fake your energy. Fix your energy. Reignite it. Protect it. Send it out like a beacon for your kind of people.

THE ENERGY YOU PUT OUT BECOMES THE BRAND

Forget branding workshops for a minute. Let's boil it down: **Your energy is your brand.** Not the font. Not the logo. Not the scripted mission statement that no one in your company actually says out loud.

Your brand is:
- How you talk in meetings.
- How you respond when something goes wrong.
- How you show up when no one's clapping yet.
- How much you care when it would be easier not to.

If you're half-assing your effort because things are slow, guess what the universe does? It sends you more half-assed clients. If you're constantly putting out scrappy, inspired, curious energy? The universe sends collaborators who want to build sh*t with you, not just "pick your brain."

That's not magic. That's coalescence.

YOU DON'T HAVE TO FAKE IT; YOU JUST HAVE TO GO FIRST

There's a difference between pretending and projecting. One is built on fear. The other is built on faith.

When you "fake it," you're secretly hoping no one notices you don't belong. When you "go first," you're sending a signal to the world: *I'm already becoming who I need to be. Catch up if you want to.*

That's leadership. That's attraction. That's how the right clients, collaborators, and opportunities find you because you showed up like the person they were looking for, even before you had the receipts.

So, don't fake confidence. Choose courage. Don't fake experience. Show vision. Don't fake your success. Define it for yourself, and walk like it's inevitable.

IF THE ENERGY IS RIGHT, THE UNIVERSE DELIVERS

You don't have to lie. You don't have to pretend. You don't have to contort yourself into a knockoff version of someone you saw killing it on LinkedIn last week. You just have to believe in what you're building, act like it already matters, and send that signal consistently in how you speak, how you sell, and how you show up.

That energy? That intention? That's the real invitation. If you radiate doubt, you'll attract noise. If you radiate purpose, you'll attract people who want to build with you.

So, no, it's not "fake it till you make it."

It's: **Act like it. Attract like it. Build like it's already real. And watch what starts to gravitate toward you.**

RULE 9

BUSY IS BULLSH*T

IF YOU'RE ALWAYS SLAMMED,
YOU'RE DOING IT WRONG

Let's get one thing straight: **Being "busy" is not a personality trait.** It's not a flex. It's not a business strategy. It's not a status symbol. It's just... a symptom.

A symptom of saying yes too often. A symptom of unclear priorities. A symptom of valuing productivity porn over actual progress. And yet, we've glorified it.

We've turned "slammed" into some kind of elite club. If you're not booked back-to-back with meetings, running on caffeine and cortisol, and answering emails at midnight, are you even trying?

Let's all say it together now: **Busy is bullsh*t.**

THE CULT OF HUSTLE (AND WHY IT NEEDS TO BE RAIDED BY THE FBI)

There's this unspoken narrative that if you're not exhausted, you're not successful. If your calendar isn't color-coded chaos, you're clearly not in demand. If you're not bragging about how you haven't taken a day off since 2018, are you even an entrepreneur?

Here's the truth of it: **Hustle culture is just burnout in a blazer.** It's performative. It's addictive. And it tricks you into thinking that movement equals momentum.

But you know what hustle culture doesn't get you?

» Space to think.

- » Time to lead.
- » Energy to create.
- » The mental clarity to say, "No, that's a terrible idea," before it ends up in a pitch deck.

Real leaders don't need to be busy. They need to be present. They need to be available for thinking, coaching, creating, and, let's not forget, living. You can't build the business of your dreams when you're just trying to survive your schedule.

MOTION IS NOT THE SAME AS PROGRESS

Let's talk about a hard truth: **You can be running full speed in the wrong direction.**

Meetings, emails, check-ins, Slack threads, project tasks, back-to-back Zoom calls where everyone's half-listening while scrolling Instagram—none of that guarantees that anything important is actually happening.

Activity ≠ effectiveness.

Volume ≠ value.

Motion ≠ momentum.

PROGRESS ISN'T ABOUT HOW MUCH YOU DO. IT'S ABOUT WHAT YOU MOVE FORWARD.

Some of the most "productive" days we've ever had ended in us staring at the ceiling, thinking, *What did we actually get done today?* And the answer was, "We updated the team on something that didn't need a meeting, rescheduled the meeting we didn't want to have, and then responded to eighty-seven messages about said meeting."

Progress isn't about how much you do. It's about what you move forward.

You don't need a 12-hour workday. You need a 30-minute block of clear-headed strategy that isn't hijacked by people asking you to approve something for the third time.

REST IS NOT A REWARD. IT'S A REQUIREMENT.

You're not a laptop. You don't need to be "plugged in" at all times. You are a human being. You need sleep. You need silence. You need time to do absolutely nothing so your brain can wander into brilliance.

But somewhere along the way, we decided rest was something you earn. That you're not allowed to stop unless you've crossed off your 37-item to-do list, solved world hunger, and replied to every message with a GIF that shows "team spirit."

Here's your new rule: **Rest isn't what you do after the work is done. It's what makes the work possible.**

You want better ideas? Go for a walk. You want more clarity? Take a nap. You want to stop being resentful of your business? Step the hell away from it sometimes.

You don't need to earn rest. You just need to stop acting like you're a machine built only for output.

THE POWER OF STRATEGIC SPACE

You know what's better than a jam-packed calendar? White space. Breathing room. A margin. That's where strategy happens. That's where ideas land. That's where your brain has time to do what it's best at—connecting dots and thinking beyond today's fire drill.

If your schedule is so full that you can't even think, that's not ambition. That's poor management. Build in time to think, plan, wander, sketch, question, and step back. Call it a "vision block" if that makes it sound fancy enough for your calendar. But protect the hell out of it.

BUSY ISN'T A BADGE. IT'S A BURDEN.

You're not here to run in circles, chasing the flag like you're qualifying for NASCAR. You're here to lead. And leadership requires perspective, which you can't get if you're buried under a pile of email threads about who still hasn't updated their bio photo.

JESUS . . . TAKE THE WHEEL

Here's a truth: **Your schedule is a mirror.**

Want to know what you really value? Look at your calendar. If it's all reactive chaos, if it's full of meetings you dread and tasks you don't even remember saying yes to, you're not running your business. Your business is running you. And probably into the ground.

So, take back the damn wheel. Say no more often. Build in recovery time. Create space for ideas, not just tasks. And for the love of your future self, stop equating "busy" with "important."

Busy isn't a badge. It's a burden.

And we didn't come this far to carry burnout around like it's a trophy.

BUSY IS A BRAG FOR PEOPLE WHO DON'T KNOW WHAT THEY WANT

Let's stop glamorizing burnout. Let's stop confusing chaos with competence. Let's stop pretending that being underwater is some noble badge of honor instead of a red flashing light that says, "Yo, fix this."

Because the goal isn't to be busy. The goal is to be effective. To be present. To be in control of your time instead of chained to your calendar like a corporate hostage.

So, here are a few truths to tattoo on your brain (or your whiteboard, or your coffee mug—you do you):

- » If your calendar looks like a game of Tetris played by a psychopath, it's time for a reset.
- » Being slammed isn't a flex. It's an operations failure.
- » If you don't protect your time, everyone else will claim it like free Wi-Fi.
- » Hustle without harmony is just burnout in activewear.
- » Busy looks impressive. Focus is impressive.
- » You don't need to be available. You need to be impactful.
- » The quietest people in the room are often the ones getting sh*t done.
- » Rest isn't lazy; it's leadership in disguise.
- » You don't need to move faster. You need to move smarter.

Your time is your most valuable currency. Spend it like someone who knows it's finite.

So, breathe. Back out of that unnecessary meeting. Put some damn white space in your week. And remember this: **You didn't build your own business just to be too busy to enjoy it.**

Let's kill the cult of busy. Let's build something better. One intentional hour at a time.

BOUNDARY-SETTING ISN'T A HACK. IT'S A WAY OF LIFE.

Look, if you're here for quick tricks and cute hacks on how to "balance better," let us save you the time: **Boundaries aren't a tactic. They're a lifestyle.**

This isn't about scheduling hacks, color-coded calendars, or inbox zero sorcery. This is about deciding who the hell you are and what the hell you're willing to tolerate. And then living and working like you mean it.

Because here are the hard truths most people avoid: Every time you say yes when you mean no, you're not being helpful; you're being dishonest. Every time you undercharge to be "nice," you're selling a piece of your soul at a discount. Every time you let that red-flag client stay on your roster because it's "just one more month," you're choosing chaos over clarity.

This is not about being hard. It's about being clear. It's about running your business and your life on purpose instead of by default.

Boundary-setting isn't about protecting your time. It's about protecting your energy. Your values. Your vision.

It's how you:

» Preserve the fire that got you into this work in the first place.
» Protect the people who said yes to following your lead.
» Repel the wrong people and attract the right ones like a human bouncer for your own damn peace of mind.

And the best part?

Once you start living like someone who sets and honors boundaries, you stop needing to enforce them all the time because people feel them. You walk differently. You speak differently. You operate from a place of calm confidence instead of constant compromise.

It's not about building walls. It's about building a business that serves your life, not the other way around.

So, let's make this real. Let's shift the standard. Let's build something that lasts without burning you out in the process.

THE TEN COMMANDMENTS OF BUSINESS BOUNDARIES: (A SACRED SCROLL FOR THE OVERBOOKED, OVERWHELMED, AND OVER IT)

And lo, on the mountaintop of burnout, the tired entrepreneur lifted their eyes to the heavens and said, "I need boundaries." And the universe replied, "Then act like it."

I. Thou Shalt Not Reply to Emails After 8 p.m.
Unless the building is literally on fire. And even then, sleep on it.

II. Thou Shalt Not Put Thy Calendar Before Thy Sanity
A full schedule is not a fulfilled life. Protect thy mornings. Block thy afternoons. Guard thy peace like a jealous raccoon.

III. Thou Shalt Not Work with Assholes
For they shall drain thy soul, curse thy team, and screw up thy timelines. Cast them out.

IV. Thou Shalt Say "No" Without a Six-Sentence Apology
"No," is a full-ass sentence. Stop decorating it.

V. Thou Shalt Price Thy Worth and Not Waver
Discounting to "get the job" is how you end up resentful and underpaid. Charge like you believe in your work because if you don't, no one else will.

VI. Thou Shalt Not Be Guilt-Tripped by "Quick Favors"
That "quick favor" costs time, energy, and a chunk of your soul. Set the boundary. Send the rate card.

VII. Thou Shalt Build a Business That Serves Thy Life, Not the Other Way Around
You are not a robot. You are not a productivity app. You're a human. Build accordingly.

VIII. Thou Shalt Not Confuse Urgency with Importance

Someone else's lack of planning is not your emergency. Breathe. Prioritize. Delay with dignity.

IX. Thou Shalt Rest Without Guilt

You do not need to earn your rest. You just need to respect yourself enough to take it.

X. Thou Shalt Remember: Boundaries Are Not Walls. They Are Invitations to Work with You Better.

Boundaries don't push people away. They show people how to respect your time, your talent, and your team the right way.

Tape these to your desk. Frame them in your office. Stitch them on a throw pillow if that's your vibe.

But whatever you do . . . keep these commandments holy. For without boundaries, there is only chaos. And calendar fatigue. And client emails that start with, "Hey, real quick . . ."

RULE 10

SKIP THE PROBLEM

BECAUSE NOT EVERY OBSTACLE DESERVES YOUR GENIUS

Let's set the scene.

You're building something from the ground up. A business, a brand, a system, a new way to do an old thing. You're solving problems daily because that's what entrepreneurs do.

You didn't sign up to just "sell stuff." You became a business owner because you wanted to solve something, maybe for your industry, maybe for your clients, or maybe for yourself. Every day, you're in it—fixing broken processes, building new services, trying to think five steps ahead and wondering if the damn printer is out of ink again.

You are not just a business owner. You are a problem solver. You're the Chief Firefighter. The Decision-Maker-in-Chief. The one with the answers, or at least the one everyone expects to find them. That means every single day, you wake up and play mental chess.

You answer questions nobody else wants to ask. You build systems nobody else understands. You stitch together vision and logistics like some demented business surgeon with duct tape and hope. You are the architect of possibility. And most days, you thrive in it.

And then it happens. You hit the problem that won't budge.

There comes a point in every builder's journey, regardless of industry, where a particular problem refuses to move. Not a hard problem. A wall problem. The kind that doesn't break down with logic. The kind that consumes your brain like a mental parasite with Wi-Fi.

> # WE'RE CONDITIONED TO BELIEVE THAT IF WE CAN'T SOLVE IT, WE'VE FAILED.

You've tried to think it to death. You've held five whiteboard sessions. You've paced the room. You've walked the dog. You've googled every version of "what to do when nothing works." And still. Nothing.

The answer won't show up. The idea won't click. The strategy won't sing. And the harder you push, the deeper the stuck becomes.

You know exactly what I mean.

That issue that keeps circling back like a mosquito with a grudge. The bottleneck that shows up in your workflow every week. The "mystery reason" the sales funnel keeps leaking. The team member who always seems just a little out of sync. The client who keeps loving the idea of your service but never quite signs on the dotted line.

It's not just frustrating. It's personal. Because we're conditioned to believe that if we can't solve it, we've failed. Especially in business. And we start believing that every problem is ours to fix. We're told to "lean in," "figure it out," "grind through it," and "pivot until you puke." Bullsh*t.

Here's what nobody says (and what I had to learn the hard way): **Sometimes, the smartest move isn't to solve the problem. It's to skip it.**

THE MOMENT IT HIT ME

There was a day I remember vividly, back when I was mentoring someone on my team. They were stuck, panicked, spiraling. Client expectations, timelines, creative block, the usual greatest hits. They were stuck, not just creatively, but existentially. They were spiraling through all the what-ifs, trying to jam a solution into a situation that just wasn't giving. I could feel the tension building and knew exactly where they were headed: into the swamp of "just keep pushing."

I listened. I nodded. And then I said something that surprised both of us:

"Skip the problem."

They blinked. So did I.

It sounded like bad advice at first. Blasphemy. Skipping problems? Isn't that irresponsible? Weak? Bad leadership? It came out of my mouth almost accidentally, like someone else said it for me. But once it was out there, I couldn't unhear it. It felt weirdly right. So, I said it again, but slower this time, like it was some ancient wisdom passed down from the business gods:

Skip. The. Problem.

It was the simplest and most profound piece of business advice I've ever stumbled across.

What I meant was this: **Stop trying to solve something that isn't solvable right now.** Because some problems are meant to redirect you, not stop you.

Not everything is a test you need to pass. Not every wall is a puzzle. Sometimes, it's just the universe blocking off a path you were never meant to walk down in the first place. So, skip it. Take the side road. Flip the board and start a new game.

What does "skip the problem" actually mean?

It doesn't mean you bury your head in the sand or ghost accountability. It doesn't mean you ignore critical issues or hope the IRS forgets your address.

> # YOU DON'T HAVE TO SOLVE EVERYTHING. YOU JUST HAVE TO KNOW WHAT'S ACTUALLY WORTH SOLVING.

"Skip the problem" means this: **If something is sucking up your time, energy, and brainpower without producing forward motion, it might not be your problem to solve right now, if at all.**

Some problems are decoys. They distract you from your real work. Some are potholes that slow you down just long enough to miss your shot. Some are tests of ego: "Can I fix this?" when the real question should be "Do I even need to?"

Entrepreneurs are wired to force it.

Most of us didn't get here by quitting. We made it because we push through. But, sometimes, our drive is the exact thing that screws us. You're exhausted, staring down a decision you've rehashed seventeen times, still thinking that one more brainstorming session will unlock the magic door. But what if that door was never meant for you? What if the energy you're burning trying to "fix it" is energy that could have built something else, something better?

You're probably fighting the wrong thing.

Here's your permission slip: **You don't have to solve everything. You just have to know what's actually worth solving.**

When you're stuck in business, whether it's a process problem, a people issue, a marketing challenge, or a service offering that feels like dragging a dead horse uphill, take a step back and ask:

» Is this actually my job to solve?
» Is this worth the energy it's costing me?
» Is there another route entirely?

Most of the time, when I've truly "skipped the problem," I didn't feel like a failure. I felt like I took off a forty-pound weighted vest I didn't know I was wearing. That's when new ideas show up. New opportunities come to mind. Simpler solutions emerge. The fix you couldn't see before becomes so obvious you actually get mad you didn't see it sooner.

SKIPPING ISN'T QUITTING—IT'S STRATEGY

You don't push through a brick wall when the window next to it is wide open. Skipping the problem isn't weak. It's wise. It means you're not burning out your team, your time, or your soul trying to brute-force your way through something that was never supposed to be the thing. You're not in business to solve everything. You're in business to solve the right things. The things that create momentum, connection, impact, and money. (In that order.)

And yes, sometimes, the problem IS you.

Let's be honest. Sometimes, the issue isn't the client or the product or the funnel. Sometimes, it's your brain. You're tired. You're overloaded. You're four decisions past your bandwidth and two coffees away from a heart palpitation.

When you're creatively, mentally, or emotionally drained, every problem looks impossible. So before you throw your laptop into traffic, do a quick self-audit: *Have I rested? Have I refueled? Am I trying to solve this with 5 percent battery left?* If so, don't skip the problem, skip the day. Go walk. Go sleep. Go live. Reset your system before you try to reset the solution.

The re-route is real.

Some of my best ideas, biggest breakthroughs, and most profitable business pivots happened not when I solved the problem but when I walked around it and discovered something entirely better waiting on the other side. So, now, anytime I hit that wall, I pause. And I ask myself: *Is this a problem to solve... or a sign to skip?*

You know what happens when you skip the problem? Your brain resets. The pressure breaks. The alternative paths show up like they were hiding behind a curtain the whole time.

NOT EVERY WALL NEEDS A BATTERING RAM.

Sometimes, I circle back and find a clearer path. Sometimes, I realize the project was missing an entirely different question. Sometimes, and this is important, I never go back. Because I find a better way, a faster route, a simpler solution. And every single time I do, I thank Past Me for not being an arrogant jackass who believed every problem must be solved with brute force.

Nine times out of ten, skipping leads me where I was actually meant to go all along. And that's not failure. That's freaking magic.

So, the next time you're stuck...

Don't panic. Don't spiral. And for the love of your business, don't go rearranging your process strategy at 3 a.m. Try this instead:

» Take a breath.
» Say the words: "Skip the problem."
» Look left, look right, look anywhere but dead ahead.
» Then, find another route.

So, if the idea won't click, the client won't budge, or the solution won't come? Take a deep breath. Flip the map around. And skip the damn problem.

Because not every wall needs a battering ram. Sometimes, you just need to look for the side door. And when you find it, you'll wonder why you ever wasted so much time trying to bust through a wall that wasn't ever gonna move anyway.

RULE 11

PICK UP THE DAMN PHONE

AND OTHER ANCIENT RITUALS FROM A TIME WHEN RELATIONSHIPS STILL MATTERED

Let me start with a confession...
There was a time when I thought email was the greatest invention in the history of business. It let me organize my thoughts. Avoid awkward conversations. Sound smarter than I actually am. And, most importantly, it let me avoid conflict without technically ignoring people.

It was perfect. Until it wasn't.

A CAUTIONARY TALE: THE COSTLY EMAIL

We once had a client. . . . let's call him Tom (because that was his name), who emailed us one Friday afternoon with what seemed like a simple message:

Hey, I had a few thoughts. Let's tweak the direction slightly. Nothing major.

Slightly. Nothing major. A few thoughts.

So, naturally, we cracked open the doc expecting a handful of light comments. What we got was a seventeen-paragraph outline written like a breakup letter from someone who had absolutely NOT been "fine."

He questioned the tone. The strategy. The fonts. He referenced an Instagram post from 2019. He cited his gut feeling about the market.

He even included a YouTube link to a motivational coach and said, *Maybe we need more of this energy.*

No further explanation. Just vibes.

Now, instead of doing what we should've done which was pick up the damn phone and talk it through like grown adults, we did what scared, busy professionals do when they're emotionally fried: We . . . emailed back.

But not just any email. Oh, no. We wrote The Great Novel of Passive Professionalism™. 1,600 words. Three sections. Links. Screenshots. We included bulleted lists and phrases like "to clarify" and "as previously discussed." We even workshopped it with the team. Sent it through Grammarly. Read it out loud to make sure we didn't sound "defensive."

WE WERE ACTUALLY BEING EMOTIONALLY UNAVAILABLE PROFESSIONALS WITH WI-FI.

It took us three hours.

We hit send. Poured a drink. Felt victorious. Maybe even high-fived each other.

Monday morning, Tom replied: *Thanks. Let's just hop on a call.*

One call. Twenty minutes. All resolved. Everyone was fine. Project saved.

The funniest part about it was that he hadn't even read our long, drawn-out email response.

All that work on crafting a response? A complete waste of time. Also, it cost us over $1,200 in billable hours internally. Plus, the therapy co-pay. But it could have cost us way more. It could have cost us a valuable client in the process.

The moral? Call. The. Client. Before you start writing your response. Before you spiral into oblivion. Before you Google "how to professionally tell someone they're sabotaging the business they hired you to save."

Pick up the phone. Save the drama. Save the energy. Save the f*cking budget. Because nine times out of ten, a call is faster, kinder, and smarter than that masterpiece you're drafting in Google Docs at midnight.

THE GREAT HIDE-AND-SEEK GAME OF BUSINESS

Email became the shield. Messenger became the substitute. And "let me circle back" became the universal code for ... I'm going to ignore this until you either forget about it or die.

We started hiding behind our screens. Sending perfectly punctuated messages to avoid the human part of doing business. We thought we were being efficient. We were actually being emotionally unavailable professionals with Wi-Fi.

And here's the part nobody warns you about: **If you avoid enough real conversations, the relationship quietly dies.** Not with a bang. With an unsubscribe.

CONVENIENCE KILLS CONNECTION

Yes, I know. You're busy. You've got back-to-backs. You're trying to keep clients happy, the team sane, and the bills paid. So, when a problem comes up, or a client's got questions, or things feel a little tense ...

You take the easy route:
» Draft an email.
» Add a few "per my last email" for flair.
» Insert a bullet-pointed list of updates.
» Slap on a "Let us know if you have any questions!"

- » Send.
- » Exhale.
- » Then, immediately mark it unread so you can deal with it later. And repeat.

You're not solving the problem. You're putting a beautifully written buffer between you and actual connection.

Spoiler: **This is how relationships die.**

The client stops feeling seen. Your team starts communicating like bots. Everything sounds like it was written by a passive-aggressive AI. And one day, the client just stops responding altogether.

No fight. No feedback. Just . . . silence.

You didn't lose them because you messed up the project. You lost them because you stopped showing up like a real human being.

THE PHONE CALL IS NOW A SUPERPOWER

Here's the wildest twist in modern business: **Calling someone is now a radical act.** It cuts through the noise. It makes things real. It says, *Hey, I'm not hiding. Let's fix this like actual adults.*

If you pick up the phone when no one else does? You become unforgettable.

You know what you can't hear in an email?

- » Tone.
- » Humor.
- » Frustration.
- » Relief.
- » The realness of another human trying to collaborate with you.

You know what you can do in a call that you can't do in an email message?

- » Build trust.
- » Diffuse tension.
- » Clarify confusion.

» Save a relationship.

You know what a client never forgets? The time you called instead of sending a templated update while they were spiraling in uncertainty.

TEXTS DON'T BUILD TRUST

This goes for quick texts, Slack DMs, carrier pigeons—all of it.

Yes, they're convenient. But you cannot build a long-term relationship on quick hits and half-hearted replies.

If all your client ever sees is:
» "Will do."
» "Got it."
» "On it."
» "Let's circle back."

Yeah, they'll eventually circle back . . . to another provider who actually gave a damn.

WHEN TO EMAIL, WHEN TO CALL, AND WHEN TO SHOW UP WITH COFFEE AND AN APOLOGY

Let's break this down in the simplest possible way:

SITUATION	ACTION
A client sends a long email with "concerns."	CALL THEM. IMMEDIATELY.
Team tension is brewing over miscommunication.	CALL. Don't let it fester.
A project goes sideways.	Call, apologize, and co-create a solution.
You're avoiding a conversation because it feels "hard."	Guess what? That's your sign to CALL.
You just landed a big win together.	Call to celebrate. Send a voice memo. Be a human.

FROM FIREFIGHTING TO FRONTLINE: HOW YOU WORK WITH PEOPLE MATTERS

Let's talk about the three species of business behavior when it comes to working with clients, teams, and even your own people: the **Reactive**, the **Proactive**, and the rare but mighty **Co-Active**.

You've definitely met all three. Hell, you've probably *been* all three. Maybe in the same week.

REACTIVE: The "Hair's on Fire" Hustler

These folks don't show up until something's broken, burning, or bleeding.

They're always a few steps behind, constantly putting out fires like an unpaid intern at a fireworks factory. Their whole vibe is *Let me know if something goes wrong*, which sounds professional until you realize that *everything* eventually goes wrong.

And when it does, reactive people scramble. They duct-tape the problem. They spin up a Zoom conference. They apologize a lot. And then they vanish again until the next emergency.

Reactives aren't bad people; they're just exhausting. Working with them feels like you're on a reality show called *Survivor: Inbox Edition*. And guess what? Clients can feel that chaos. So can your team. Nobody sleeps easy when they know the fire department only shows up after the building's halfway gone.

PROACTIVE: The Eagle Scout of Business

These are the overachievers. The spreadsheet whisperers. The contingency plan ninjas.

Proactive folks *anticipate*. They plan. They pack snacks *and* a backup charger. They're thinking two quarters ahead and spotting potential landmines before you even know you're on a battlefield. And honestly? They're impressive. Clients love them. Teams lean on them. Everything runs smoother when proactive energy is in the room.

But here's the catch: **Proactive is still a little lonely.** It's about staying ahead, not *together*. And even the best proactive efforts can feel like guesswork if they're not plugged into the client's actual heartbeat.

That's where the magic of CO-ACTIVE kicks in.

CO-ACTIVE: The Down-the-Street Dream Partner

Now we're talking.

Co-Active is when you're not just reacting *after* something happens or trying to guess what *might* happen—you're in it *together*, building and navigating in real time. You're not just the hired help anymore. You're the confidante. The partner. The one who's not just down the hall; you're down the street, in their corner, walking the same road, reading the same room.

You're on the Zoom call, yes, but you're also texting them mid-launch to say, *Hey, just spotted this. Want me to jump in?* You're part of the heartbeat. You're building with them, not just for them.

That's what creates loyalty. That's what builds referrals. That's what turns "just another vendor" into "we can't do this without you."

Co-active relationships are stronger, deeper, and built for the long haul. Because they're not based on fear (reactive) or just good intentions (proactive). They're based on *real trust and real time*.

So, stop reacting. Don't just plan. Get in the trenches. Show up like someone who gives a damn. Pick up the phone, hop on the call, get in the room. Because when the real work happens *with* them, not *after* or *ahead* of them, that's when the work actually works.

DON'T LET CONVENIENCE RUIN WHAT YOU BUILT

This isn't just about communication style. It's about presence. It's about not letting a business full of real people get reduced to project dashboards and "touch base" emails. It's about making sure the people you work with feel you, not just receive you. So, the next time you reach for the keyboard to type a 500-word apology email . . .

Don't.

THE DEATH OF RELATIONSHIPS IS QUIET. BUT THE REVIVAL? THAT'S LOUD.

Pick up the damn phone. Or, better yet, meet with them face to face. Be brave. Be human. Be heard. And if you need a script to start the call? Try this: "Hey . . . I figured this was better than a long email. I care about this, and I want to get it right."

Boom. You just did more than most businesses do in six months of automated follow-ups.

YOU CAN'T AUTOMATE RELATIONSHIPS

Your business will never rise above the quality of your communication. And if all you ever give people is convenience? They'll start treating you like a commodity. But if you show up? If you bring voice, presence, empathy, and energy? You'll be irreplaceable.

So, call. Connect. Confront. Clarify. Celebrate.

Whatever it is, do it in real time.

The death of relationships is quiet. But the revival? That's loud.

It sounds like a phone ringing. Pick it up.

RULE 12

IF IT'S NOT A HELL YES, IT'S A HELL NO

BECAUSE "EH, MAYBE" IS A ONE-WAY TICKET TO REGRETVILLE

There is a small, magical, underappreciated voice inside every business owner. It doesn't come with a data dashboard. It doesn't have a KPI. It never shows up on the P&L. But when it speaks, you feel it in your bones.

It's your gut. Your instinct. Your internal bullsh*t detector. Your quiet little Yoda who whispers, *This is a bad idea wrapped in a decent email.*

And most of us? We ignore it.

Because the client has money. Because the opportunity might go somewhere. Because we don't want to hurt someone's feelings. Because we don't want to seem "difficult" or "ungrateful" or, God forbid, "unprofessional." So, we say yes when we should say hell no. We "circle back" instead of shutting it down. We "give it a shot" even though our instinct is waving red flags like a NASCAR pit crew.

Let's cut the crap: **If it's not a hell yes, then it's a hell no.**

GUILT IS NOT A BUSINESS STRATEGY

How many times have you said yes out of guilt?
- » "They're a friend of a friend."
- » "They're really nice."
- » "They're a startup and don't have a budget, but the vision is cool."

- » "I don't want to burn a bridge."
- » "It's not that bad."
- » "It's only temporary."
- » "What if I regret saying no?"

Meanwhile, your gut is backstage shouting, *YOU'RE GONNA REGRET SAYING YES!* But you override it. Again.

And then two months later, you're:

- » In a contract you hate.
- » Working weekends you never agreed to.
- » Being micromanaged by someone who thinks Canva makes them a creative director.
- » And resenting your past self with the intensity of a thousand suns.

Your instinct is not trying to ruin your business. It's trying to protect it. From regret. From chaos. From unaligned, low-vibe energy-sucking situations dressed up like opportunity.

INTUITION ISN'T WOO-WOO. IT'S WISDOM WITH A TRACK RECORD.

Here's what no one tells you: **Your gut is smarter than your fear.**

It may not use charts or spreadsheets or wear a power blazer, but it has receipts . . . every moment you knew something wasn't right but couldn't explain why. Every time you walked into a meeting and thought, *Nope*. Every time you said yes and immediately felt sick about it. Every time you ignored the feeling and ended up eating three bags of potato chips over the sink while venting to your dog.

Your gut isn't random. It's a pattern recognition machine. It's experience. It's instinct. It's every time you've been burned and learned. It's the part of you that has no time for politeness when your peace is on the line. You want to be a better business owner? Stop negotiating with your gut and start listening to it.

THE INTUITION TEST: LEARNING TO TRUST THE "OFF" FEELING

Let me introduce you to my business partner: part strategist, part human lie detector, and part Jedi-level gut-check machine.

She has this almost spooky ability to sense when something's off. A new client with perfect credentials but a weird vibe? She catches it. A project that looks great on paper but has red flags buried under the surface? She feels it before we even open the proposal.

At first, I brushed it off. Chalked it up to her "being cautious." But I'll admit, more times than not, she was dead right. Not just about people, but timing, partnerships, deals, you name it. If something felt off, it usually was. And now? When she gives me that look and says, *I don't like this*, I don't argue. I listen.

It's not magic. It's instinct. And it's one of the most underappreciated assets in business.

Here's what I've learned:

1) **Gut Checks Are Data Too**

Just because it's not on a spreadsheet doesn't mean it's not real. Intuition is data, but the kind you feel in your bones instead of read in a report. If someone on your team has a gut reaction to a project or person, don't wave it off. Ask why. Even if they can't explain it fully yet. Trust is built when we validate that kind of internal radar. Most bad decisions were once gut checks that got ignored.

2) **You Don't Need a Reason to Say No**

In business, we've been trained to justify every no. To explain it, rationalize it, defend it with charts and logic. But here's the truth: **"It just doesn't feel right" is enough.**

It's not indecisiveness. It's discernment. You don't need to defend your peace to people who won't protect it.

3) Instinct Is a Muscle—Use It

The more you listen to your instincts, the sharper they get. The more you ignore them, the quieter they become. Start paying attention. When did something feel wrong before it blew up? When did you ignore your gut and regret it later? Track the patterns. Build the muscle. Because your instincts, when sharpened and trusted, will become the most accurate compass in your decision-making toolkit.

4) Some People Sense the "No" So You Can Say the "Yes"

Every team needs someone who can call out the misalignment before it becomes mayhem. Sometimes, it's you. Sometimes, it's your partner, your ops lead, your assistant, your spouse. When they speak up, listen.

Your hell yes should be a shared one. If someone who's in the trenches with you isn't feeling it, that matters. Don't bulldoze past it. Slow down. Check in. Their clarity might save you from a very expensive detour.

5) The Right Opportunity Will Feel Right for Everyone

Alignment doesn't just mean money, scope, or fit. It means energy. It means trust. It means feeling right—across your leadership, your team, and your body. When your people are pausing, you should too. The best opportunities don't make you second-guess your values or your peace. They don't require "gut override" mode. They just click.

So, follow the "flinch."

The next time something feels off, even if everything looks great on paper, pause. Don't gaslight your own gut. You don't need to explain it to everyone. You just need to respect it. That hesitation? That pause? That internal flinch? It's not fear. It's foresight.

And if your team has a human radar system like my business partner, thank the universe and use it often. It just might be the difference between a business you like and a business that doesn't make you want to burn it all down and open an ice cream stand on the beach in Jamaica.

Trust in the flinch.

MAKING BOLD CALLS FASTER

Here's what happens when you start honoring your hell yes or hell no radar:
- » You stop dragging things out.
- » You stop justifying bad fits.
- » You stop over-explaining your decisions to people who don't even get it.
- » You free up time, energy, and resources for the right things.

Indecision is a momentum killer. Overthinking is a full-time job that doesn't pay well. The faster you can trust yourself, the faster you can move—with alignment, not anxiety.

NO ISN'T REJECTION. IT'S PROTECTION.

Is this scary at first? Absolutely. Especially if you're a people-pleaser, recovering over-committer, or someone raised in a corporate environment where "trusting your gut" was filed under "career-limiting behavior." But over time, saying no gets easier. And saying yes gets louder. Because your yes comes from confidence, not desperation. And your no? That's your boundary in action.

NO = PROTECTION, YES = POWER

When you say no to the wrong things, here's what you're actually saying yes to:
- » Your time
- » Your energy
- » Your sanity
- » Your team's well-being
- » Your actual goals
- » The future version of you who won't have to clean up the mess

No isn't rejection. It's protection. And when you get real good at saying no without guilt? Your yeses get way more powerful. They become full-body, aligned, soul-driven YES, YES, YES! moments that actually move your business forward. Because the stuff that deserves your yes? It doesn't feel like pressure. It feels like expansion.

YOU ALREADY KNOW. ACT LIKE IT.

Deep down, you already know what to say yes to. You already know who's a red flag. You already know which project lights you up and which one's going to make you want to fake a family emergency.

TRUST THAT WHAT'S MEANT FOR YOU DOESN'T NEED TO BE BEGGED, CHASED, OR JUSTIFIED.

Just stop. Stop pretending you don't know. Stop overcomplicating it. Stop letting fear wear the suit while intuition waits outside in the parking lot. If it's not a hell yes, it's a no. Simple. Bold. Clean. Freeing. Say it out loud. Let it ring. Let it protect your peace. And trust that what's meant for you doesn't need to be begged, chased, or justified. Your gut isn't guessing. It's guiding.

THE GUT KNOWS. THE BRAIN OVERTHINKS.

Let's bring it home.

TRUST THIS:
- » Your instinct is wiser than your inner people-pleaser.
- » "Meh" is a red flag in a trench coat.
- » A fast no beats a slow, regret-filled yes every time.
- » If your stomach tightens when you read the email, don't sign the contract.
- » Your gut already knows. You just need to quit arguing with it.

STOP DOING THIS:
- » Saying yes because you feel bad
- » Confusing obligation with alignment
- » Believing every opportunity is a "once-in-a-lifetime" shot
- » Dismissing your own discomfort because the money's decent
- » Creating a twelve-step decision-making process when your gut said no at step one

Remember: **If it's not a hell yes, it's a "please don't waste my time."** Say no more often. Say yes louder. And let your intuition run the room. The goal isn't to be agreeable. The goal is to be aligned. And trust me, nothing bad ever comes from trusting your gut. But plenty of chaos shows up when you ignore it.

Let's move. Let's trust. Let's say hell yes to what's next. (And say hell no to everything that isn't.)

RULE 13

STOP TRYING TO PROVE YOUR WORTH

YOU'RE NOT A GROUPON DEAL IN A POWERPOINT SUIT

L et's rip this Band-Aid off up top: **If you're still trying to prove your worth, you're already undercharging.**

You're not in business to "convince" people of your value like a door-to-door vacuum salesman in 1983. You're not in business to win people over with 47-page proposals, free strategy calls, and six rounds of "just a few tweaks." You're not in business to be everyone's bargain.

You're in business to deliver value. Confidently. Clearly. Consistently. Not to dance for it. Beg for it. Or water it down to make it easier for other people to swallow.

So, let's be real: **Your value isn't tied to your hours. It's tied to your impact.** And impact doesn't clock in at 9 and log out at 5.

THE HOURLY RATE LIE

Early in business, most of us make the same mistake: We price ourselves like we work at a drive-thru. And not even a decent drive-thru.

"Okay, you want branding? That'll be three hours, two mood boards, and a medium fry. Do you want a rush order for an extra $25?"

Why do we do that? Because we're scared. Because we're told to "start small." Because somewhere, someone made us believe that time spent = value delivered.

That's adorable. And totally wrong.

Because guess what? The better you are, the less time it takes you to do something. That makes you worth more, not less.

THE ENGINEER STORY (AKA: THE $50,000 "X")

Let's talk about that story. You've probably heard it before, or some iteration, but it deserves a dramatic retelling:

A massive manufacturing company had a machine that powered an entire line, and it broke. Every day the line was down, they were losing millions of dollars. After days of wrestling with the problem, their in-house engineers couldn't figure it out.

So, they call in this old retired guy—the whisperer of machines. He walks in, listens to the entire line for a few minutes, asks for a ladder, climbs up, pulls out a piece of chalk, and puts a giant red "X" on the side of one specific piece of equipment.

"This is your problem right here. Replace that piece, and it'll be fixed."

The engineer leaves. They replace the piece of equipment that he told them. Miraculously, the machine roars back to life, and profits are saved. Woohoo. The CEO celebrates with a cocktail on the golf course.

A few days later, the company gets a bill: $50,000.

Sure, they were losing millions for days. What's $50,000 to them? Pocket change. That guy just saved their butts for their next stakeholders meeting. Then, the CEO sees the bill. Outraged, since the engineer had only spent a few minutes in their facility, the CEO asked for an itemized invoice.

Here's what the engineer sends back:

1) **Travel time/on-site assessment: $1,000**
2) **Knowing where to put the X: $49,000**

Boom.

Because the value wasn't in the labor. It was in the wisdom. The precision. The expertise born from years of experience. How much was that worth?!

> **MOST OF US DON'T UNDERCHARGE BECAUSE WE DON'T KNOW OUR VALUE. WE UNDERCHARGE BECAUSE WE'RE ADDICTED TO BEING LIKED.**

So, unless you're charging for that level of insight—not time—you're selling yourself like you're running a lemonade stand and not a professional operation.

There's the financial side of business, and then there's the experience economy. Understand your value in each of these. Know your worth.

APPROVAL IS A HELL OF A DRUG

Let's get honest for a minute. Most of us don't undercharge because we don't know our value. We undercharge because we're addicted to being liked.

"If I make it affordable, they'll like me."

"If I say yes to this scope, they'll trust me."

"If I push back, they won't refer me."

"If I do a great job, they'll validate my entire existence and maybe even hug me in public."

Yikes.

Here's the truth bomb: **People-pleasing is just insecurity in a customer service voice.**

You don't need their approval. You need alignment. You need respect. You need to walk into every room (or Zoom) knowing you don't have to prove a damn thing. You are not a puppy auditioning for a treat. You are the expert. Own it.

STOP JUSTIFYING, START OWNING

Ever find yourself sending a quote and immediately following it up with seventeen paragraphs explaining why they should hire you and why it's "actually a great deal"? That's not confidence. That's fear in business casual.

If your offer is rooted in real value, say the number and shut up.

No one needs your inner monologue. No one asked for your pricing insecurities. No one needs your *I know this might seem high, but I promise I'll overdeliver!* disclaimer.

You're not in court. You're not in therapy. You're in business. Deliver value. Back it up with results. Price it like a grown-up. Let them decide if it's a yes. You don't need to beg. You're not on Shark Tank. I'd rather lose five projects at $2,000 and focus on the one at $20,000.

PRICE LIKE AN ICON, NOT AN INTERN

Let's get one thing straight: **Your pricing isn't just about what you do.** It's about who you are, how long it took you to become this good, and what it costs to keep that creative brain of yours functioning on all cylinders without imploding from a dozen half-priced client "opportunities."

You think Apple sets its prices based on the number of hours Tim Cook spends soldering tiny chips with a magnifying glass? Hell no. They price based on the billions they've poured into product R&D, their market dominance, their design legacy, and the fact that they know people will drop $1,200 on a phone they'll mostly use to doom-scroll TikTok and ignore calls from unknown numbers.

Your R&D is no different.

It just looks like all-nighters, decades of practice, expensive trial-and-error, and enough coffee-fueled meltdowns to qualify as an Olympic sport.

That history? That craftsmanship? That's your value. That's what your pricing should reflect, not just the time you spent thinking, planning, or developing content, but the years it took to get so damn good that you make it look easy.

THE PRICING EPIPHANY (OR: THAT ONE TIME WE SWEATED THROUGH OUR SHIRTS)

Years ago, back when I was an exec at a marketing firm, pricing projects felt like standing in front of a firing squad. Every time we quoted something, I had this nagging voice in the back of my head whispering, *Is this too much? Are we really worth this?*

So, we did what most people do. We justified it. We calculated hours, added up costs, wrote out task lists, and hoped the final number wouldn't make a client laugh us out of the building.

Then, one day, we brought in a consultant. Enter Trey. He was a successful businessman with a taste for Grand Marnier, a closet full of very expensive shoes, and zero tolerance for bullsh*t. He asked us to walk him through our contract pricing model. We showed him our carefully crafted spreadsheets and told him how we estimated project costs based on time, hard expenses, and a sprinkle of blind optimism.

He looked at it like we'd just handed him a third grader's science fair volcano. Then came the questions.

"How many years did you go to school to learn this?"

"How long have you been doing this work?"

"How much did your laptop cost? Your software? Your camera gear?"

"How many hours a week do you spend thinking, strategizing, absorbing, and creating, even when you're not 'on the clock'?"

We answered.

Then, he leaned in and said, "Cool. Now triple your prices." Cue the full-body sweat.

We laughed awkwardly. We panicked quietly. But we listened, and we trusted him. After all, he did have really nice shoes, and, at this point, my Reeboks' soles were about to fall off.

So, we changed the pricing model. We started charging based on value and experience, not just hours and outputs. And when our next pitch came around, we walked into that meeting sweating bullets, but we held the line. We didn't justify. We didn't talk about how many design rounds it took or what tools we'd use. We talked about the years of collective expertise. The strategic thinking. The tactics we'd honed over the years. The roster of clients we'd had success with. And the high-impact results we bring to the table.

The client nodded. Smiled. And signed on the spot.

They didn't flinch. They didn't ask for a discount. And they didn't request a line-item breakdown.

Holy sh*t, it felt good.

We walked out, shut the car doors, screamed like teenagers, and popped champagne that night. And from that moment forward, we never looked back.

YOU'RE NOT A FAST-FOOD COMBO. YOU'RE A F*CKING TASTING MENU.

YOUR R&D IS PRICELESS, SO CHARGE ACCORDINGLY

Listen, if Apple can charge $5,000 for a laptop that has two ports and no escape key, you can charge more than you're currently charging.

You've spent years fine-tuning your instincts. You've failed, adapted, and reinvented. You've built processes, a reputation, and a point of view. That's your intellectual capital. That's your R&D.

When you price like a service technician, you attract buyers who treat you like it. When you price like a visionary, you attract people who want to partner with one. And if a client doesn't see the value? Let them go haggle with the Fiverr crowd. You're not a fast-food combo. You're a f*cking tasting menu.

Here's the bold truth: **YOU are the X.**

Let's go back to that engineer story one more time because here's the twist: You're not charging for your time. You're charging for the X. And you are the damn X. You're the one who's poured in the years. Who's made mistakes. Who's studied, tested, refined, learned, and unlearned. You've earned your price.

So, stop selling your minutes. Start selling your magic.

PRICE LIKE YOU GIVE A DAMN ABOUT YOURSELF

You don't have to justify your worth. You have to own it. Live it. Say it out loud: in numbers, in posture, in tone. If they don't get it? They're not your people. But when you price with confidence, you send a signal to the universe that you're not playing small anymore. To your future clients that you're not here to be bartered with like a used toaster. To yourself that you finally get it. And that changes everything.

YOUR VALUE ISN'T DEFINED BY WHAT YOU CHARGE. IT'S DEFINED BY HOW YOU SHOW UP.

So, charge like you know where to put the X. Because you do.
You're the damn value.

Let's be crystal clear: **You're not overcharging. You've just been undervaluing yourself for so long that fair pricing feels radical.** Let's fix that.

Say this to yourself:
» "I'm not selling hours. I'm selling outcomes."
» "If they want cheap, they can scroll Fiverr until their soul gives out."
» "I'm not here to prove anything. I'm here to partner, solve, and elevate."
» "I charge what this is worth because I know what it's worth."
» "I'm the one who knows where to put the X."
» "My pricing is not up for negotiation. It's up for alignment."

Let go of:
» The need to justify every line item
» The temptation to "just discount this one"
» The anxiety spiral that hits right after you send a quote

- » The fear of rejection disguised as "being reasonable"
- » The voice in your head that says, Who do you think you are?

Remember: **They're not just paying for your time. They're paying for the years it took to get this good.** Proving your worth is a full-time job for people who forgot they already have value. You don't need every client. You need the right ones. And if they don't respect your price? That's not a red flag. That's a gift-wrapped exit.

Charge like you give a damn about your work. Then, deliver like the pro you are. No more dancing. No more discounting. No more pretending you're "just happy to be here." You're not here to beg. You're here to build.

FINAL THOUGHT: YOU DON'T HAVE TO PROVE IT—JUST PRACTICE IT

Let's get one thing straight: **This isn't a chapter about how to slap an extra zero on your invoice** just because you watched a video or read a book about self-worth. It's not about playing the pricing game like it's Monopoly and hoping nobody notices you're charging more for Baltic Avenue.

Your value isn't defined by what you charge. It's defined by how you show up.

Can you (and should you) price your work to reflect the experience, insight, and results you bring? Hell yes. But real worth isn't always attached to a price tag.

Sometimes, it looks like:

- » Holding your ground with kindness
- » Listening when someone's in panic mode and needs to unload
- » Delivering early without announcing it with fanfare
- » Offering creative advice that helps a client even when it's "not in the scope"
- » Saying no when you know it's not right and doing it with respect

- » Showing up when you didn't have to
- » Letting someone else take the spotlight because it means more to them
- » Giving people your attention, not just your output

We don't do these things for applause. We do them because they build long-term equity. Not the financial kind. The human kind.

You get what you give. And if you only give what someone paid for? That's not your worth. That's just slavery with extra steps. (Shoutout to Rick and Morty for that mic drop of truth.)

But here's the trick: **When you know your worth, you don't have to prove it every time.** You just have to live it. Consistently. Quietly. Confidently.

Remember that massive client from chapter 1? The one we had to fire with grace because they were sucking the soul out of the team? We didn't slam the door on the way out. We didn't blast them on Twitter or talk negatively about them to others. We didn't send a passive-aggressive invoice titled "EMOTIONAL DAMAGE." We just stepped away. With peace. With kindness. But with a line drawn in the sand.

And you know what happened? Years later, they came back. Not because we were cheaper. Not because we begged. But because we treated them with dignity, even when they were acting like caffeinated toddlers with a corporate card. They remembered our patience. Our professionalism. Our refusal to be petty. And they respected that.

Here's the secret: **When you stop performing for validation and start operating from grounded worth, people feel it.** You become the calm in the room. The one they trust. The one they call when it matters most. Not because you shouted your value. But because you lived it.

So, stop trying to prove your worth. Start practicing it. Over time, the right people will see it. And the wrong ones? They'll either grow or go. Either way, you win.

Now go send that invoice—just don't forget to build in some grace.

THE PRICING MANIFESTO: (SAY IT WITH YOUR CHEST AND SEND THE INVOICE)

We do not charge for hours. We charge for expertise, vision, and the clarity to know what the hell we're doing.

We believe:
- Discounting isn't humility. It's hesitation.
- "Affordable" is not a personality trait.
- We are not "budget-friendly." We are results-friendly.
- Our work solves problems, moves people, and builds brands. That sh*t costs money.
- Confidence is part of the service. If you're not ready to own your price, no one else will.

We do not:
- Break our own boundaries just to get the job.
- Apologize for not being "cheap."
- Compete on price with folks who copy Canva templates and call it branding.
- Add three free things to a proposal "just to justify the price."
- Lower the amount just because someone said their cousin could do it cheaper. (Let your cousin do it. Good luck.)

We do:
- Know what it costs to do this well.
- Show up fully, charge accordingly, and deliver the damn magic.
- Work with clients who get it.
- Raise our rates as our skills rise.
- Sleep well because we're not resenting our invoices anymore.

This is not ego.

This is alignment. This is integrity. This is respect for our time, our talent, and our teams. And if that scares off the wrong people?

Good.

Drop this in your onboarding guide. Stick it on your keyboard. Whisper it to your mirror every Monday. Whatever you do . . . don't forget who the hell you are and what you're worth.

RULE 14

PROTECT YOUR POWER SOURCE

BECAUSE BURNOUT DOESN'T KNOCK—IT BREAKS THE DOOR DOWN

If you want to build a business that lasts, you better learn how to protect your power source.

Not your company. Not your pricing. You.

Your energy. Your mind. Your creativity. Your gut. Your freaking life force. Because here's the deal: **A business doesn't run on hustle. It runs on human power.** And if that power isn't protected? You can scale, optimize, automate, and delegate your way straight into a full-on breakdown.

WHAT USES POWER ISN'T THE PROBLEM. IT'S WHAT STEALS IT.

Look, doing great work takes energy. So does leading a team. So does writing emails, taking meetings, and making hard-ass decisions every day. That's all normal. That's all investment.

What's not okay is when your energy is leaking like a cracked battery constantly being siphoned by stuff you never even see coming:

- » People who low-key stress you out even when they're "nice"
- » Projects that drag on because no one wants to say it's gone off-track
- » Toxic culture that pings your nervous system all day
- » "Quick feedback" that feels more like a trust erosion exercise
- » Constant urgency that's really just bad planning in a panic hat

These are silent drains, small enough to ignore in the moment, dangerous enough to kill your power over time.

YOUR POWER BANK HAS LIMITS

You don't notice it right away. At first, it just takes a little longer to get excited. Then, your ideas stop flowing. Then, you start resenting the people you used to love working with. Then, you're exhausted by 2 p.m.—not from the work, but from navigating the emotional landmines of your business.

Eventually? You crash. The battery's gone. The spark is out. You don't need a nap; you need a resurrection.

The worst part about this? The power drain isn't just from what you do. It's from what you never get to do. That deep, focused work that actually fuels you? Yeah, it's buried under an avalanche of admin.

ENERGY ISN'T JUST SPENT. IT NEEDS TO BE REFILLED.

Here's what they never taught you in business school: **Energy is currency, and you better budget it like a savage.**

You have to know:
» What drains you (and who)
» What recharges you (and when)
» And how long you can operate before your power bank needs a serious reboot

For example:

THINGS THAT DRAIN:
» Endless revisions for a client who'll never be happy
» Over-scheduled days with no "creative" space
» Leading without support
» Pretending to care when you don't
» Projects that don't align with your values but "pay well" (aka: the soul tax)

THINGS THAT CHARGE:
- » Real conversations with visionary clients
- » Unstructured time to think, wander, and breathe
- » Making something just because it excites you
- » Saying no and not explaining yourself
- » Leading your team with clarity and courage

You'll never eliminate all the drains. That's not the goal. The goal is awareness. Because once you start tracking where your energy actually goes, you start getting ruthless about what (and who) deserves it.

POWER IS REPLENISHABLE—BUT ONLY IF YOU PROTECT IT

If you wait until you're fried, anxious, uninspired, and watching reruns of your own exit strategy to do something about your energy? It's already too late.

The best businesses are not run by the most talented people. They're run by the people who've learned to protect their power like it's sacred. Because it is.

So:
- » Audit your energy like it's money.
- » Say no like your peace depends on it.
- » Schedule the recharge like a meeting with your highest-paying client.
- » Cut what kills your spark.
- » And stop apologizing for needing protection from your own schedule.

Because once your battery is gone, so is the business you actually love.

THE RESET YOU DIDN'T KNOW YOU NEEDED

Let me take you back to November 14, 1969, the height of the space race. Apollo 11 had successfully landed on the moon, and now the next mission was on deck.

Countdown and then blast off. Apollo 12 roared ahead, but had barely cleared the launch pad when, just thirty-six seconds into its ride to the moon, the spacecraft took not one, but two direct hits from lightning as if the universe was testing its resolve with a pair of cosmic haymakers.

Instant chaos.

The lights on the command module's control panel went berserk. Every alarm that could go off did. Inside Mission Control, the best minds in the world stared at data that appeared like a psychedelic fever dream. Telemetry readings flatlined. It looked like the mission was going down before it even left the neighborhood.

Then came one of the coolest moments in NASA lore. A flight controller named John Aaron, a twenty-four-year-old engineer with ice in his veins, remembered an obscure power setting from a past simulator run. Without any hesitation, he leaned into his headset and calmly said:

"Flight, try SCE to AUX."

Now, to the untrained ear, that sounds like Star Trek technobabble. To the Apollo crew? It was an improbable lifeline.

They flipped the switch, Signal Conditioning Equipment to Auxiliary. In a miracle moment, the system's power settings and scrambled data streams snapped back to life. Instruments came back online. The operation wasn't lost after all. This obscure, almost forgotten tactic saved not only the mission but the lives of the astronauts who had run out of options.

Why This Matters More Than You Think

Most people read this story and think, "Wow, space is crazy." But the real lesson is universal: When the lightning hits your launch, you don't need to fight the storm. You don't need to panic. You just need to hit the reset button.

In your business, your life, and your work, you're going to get struck. Not might. You will. Sometimes twice in thirty-six seconds. You'll lose your power. You'll see red alerts blinking on every dashboard you depend on—your calendar, your bank account, your energy, and your patience.

And when that happens, most of us panic. We press every button, hoping something works. We spiral. We call meetings. We try to control what can't be controlled. But the people who thrive aren't the ones who fight the chaos. They're the ones who know how to flip their own SCE to AUX.

Your Power System Needs a Reset, Too

The point of the story: You are Apollo 12. Life is the lightning.

The bad client, the impossible deadline, the fifty-email thread about whether your decisions should go left or right . . . they're the strikes that fry your systems. Most of us are wired to try and power through. We keep staring at the smoking dashboard, hoping the alarms will stop on their own. We waste time rehashing the cascading problem instead of doing what we should do—resetting the system.

Sometimes, maybe even most of the time, you don't need to fix the storm. You need to flip your own damn SCE to AUX.

What flipping your switch looks like:

1) **Pause the panic.**

When everything's crashing down, your first instinct is to do something—anything—as fast as possible. Don't. Chaos feeds on urgency like a troll under a bridge. Stop. Close your eyes. Take three deep, deliberate breaths. Remind yourself that you're not being chased by a tiger. You're just facing a problem that needs a cooler head. Always remember this: Chaos never rewards urgency.

2) **Do one small thing you know works.**

Overwhelmed brains get paralyzed. Break the freeze by taking a single, concrete action that's well within your control. Send the email that's been haunting your draft folder. Clean your workspace until it doesn't look like a raccoon ransacked it. Or just refill your water bottle. Momentum loves small wins.

3) **Reset your environment.**

Stuck in a mental fog? Your physical surroundings could be the culprit. Change your scenery. If you're slumped at your desk, stand up and stretch like a semi-pro yoga instructor. Switch rooms, head to a coffee shop, or even just face a different direction. Play music that shifts your mood: metal, jazz, whale sounds, whatever yanks you out of your funk.

4) **Interrupt the downward spiral.**

When your thoughts start circling the drain, you need an outside voice to pull you out. Call your own "John Aaron," that friend, partner, or mentor who can say, "You're fine. Here's what you actually need to do." Bonus points if they make you laugh, because humor is like emotional Drano for your clogged head.

My business partner has a great way of helping me when I spiral. She simply says, "Drink your juice, Shelby." (That's for all the Steel Magnolias fans out there.) Yes, it's random, but it somehow works.

5) **Rest.**

Your productivity heroics won't fix anything if your brain is running on fumes. The easiest, cheapest, most effective SCE to AUX reset? A nap. Even a short rest can reset your mood, your clarity, and your ability to not send that rage-fueled email draft. Sleep isn't weakness. It's your body's built-in reboot button. Let's call this the "Four-Hour Work Sleep™."

Don't Let a Lightning Strike Sink Your Mission

Lightning will hit you. Life will short-circuit your focus. Business will zap your power source just when you're trying to launch something big. But remember: **The problem isn't the storm. It's refusing to flip the switch.**

So next time your systems are overloaded, alarms blaring, and you're questioning every decision you've ever made, channel your inner John Aaron: Switch SCE to AUX. Reset your power. And get back to the mission.

The measure of your resilience isn't whether you can avoid the strikes; it's how quickly you reset when they do. Because your best work isn't done in the panic. It's done after the reset.

So, "Drink your juice, Shelby."

THE SPARK TEST (OR AS I CALL IT, THE *"HELL YES"* LITMUS)

We've talked a lot about what drains your power source, but let's talk a bit about the parts of our business that infuse us with power.

>You want a surefire way to check whether a new project, client, or opportunity is worth your time?

Picture this: You see their name pop up on your phone or in your inbox. Do you groan? Do you immediately start mentally drafting your "Sorry, we're full" response? Or do you feel that flicker, that subtle surge in your gut that says, "Yes. This is it. Let's go."

That's your spark talking. It doesn't shout. It nudges. It taps on your shoulder with a grin and says, *This could be fun.*

The older your business gets, the more your nervous system becomes the best project manager on your team. So, stop silencing it. If it lights you up? Explore it. If it drags you down? Let it go, or delegate it like it's radioactive.

ONCE YOUR BATTERY IS GONE, SO IS THE BUSINESS YOU ACTUALLY LOVE.

Because power isn't about how many things you can do. It's about how often you can stay connected to the work that actually makes you feel powerful.

Here's a fun little experiment to try:

Start color-coding everything: your emails, your messages, your tasks, and your calendar. Ruthlessly audit your week. Color-code the sh*t out of it.

Green = energizing

Red = soul-sucking

Yellow = neutral . . . but could slide either way depending on your caffeine intake that morning.

You'll start to see what's siphoning your energy away. Once you see the patterns, get savage. Delete the red. Guard the green. Find ways to shift the yellow into the green. Or manage it out.

Reclaim your bandwidth like it's stolen treasure.

WHEN THE WORK GIVES YOU GOOSEBUMPS

Let's talk about that moment. You know the one.

You're deep in it. You've lost track of time. You're not second-guessing, overthinking, or trying to sound smart. You're just making something, and suddenly, it hits.

A chill runs down your spine. You get goosebumps. You sit back and whisper to no one in particular: "Oh, sh*t. This is it."

That's not hype. **That's frisson** (pronounced free-sawn if you want to sound fancy at dinner parties). Yes, it's a real term. Look it up. It's a French term, and it means "shiver" or "thrill."

Frisson is that sudden, involuntary chill that runs up your spine when something hits you just right. It's a full-body *hell yes*. A quick, electric jolt from your nervous system that says, *Whatever this is, it matters.*

Science says it's "a neurochemical response to emotionally powerful stimuli, often triggered by music, art, or moments of awe."[1]

Translation: It's your body throwing a rave when your soul recognizes something powerful just showed up.

This isn't just a cool feeling. It's not a coincidence. It's not caffeine. It's not adrenaline. It's what happens when something actually connects—when your work doesn't just exist; it vibrates on a frequency that even your skin picks up on. You know that feeling.

It's feedback from the universe. An undeniable, full-body green light that says: *Whoa . . . whatever you're doing right now? Keep doing it.*

You're not just checking off a box. You're not just filling a scope of work. You're channeling something. Your ideas feel like they're coming from somewhere deeper. The words hit faster. The visuals click harder. Time bends. Doubt disappears. Everything feels sharp, focused, and alive.

Frisson.

That's what it feels like to be in the sweet spot where skill meets instinct and passion meets execution. It's when you're not grinding

---

1 "Frisson," *Wikipedia*, last modified June 2025, accessed July 13, 2025, https://en.wikipedia.org/wiki/Frisson.

anymore. You're gliding. You're not just working. You're transmitting. Like a live wire plugged straight into the source.

It's energy in its purest form, and it's rare as hell. Learn to recognize it. Resonate with it. And protect it at all costs.

THE BEST METRIC FOR GREAT WORK IS WHETHER IT MAKES YOU FEEL SOMETHING.

Some people spend their whole lives chasing success and never once touch that feeling. They hit revenue goals but never reverberate with that kind of energy. They get applause but never get that internal surge that makes your hair stand up and your skin tingle.

When you hit that zone, you know you're not just doing the work. You've become the conduit. The work is flowing through you, not just around you. It's a reminder that you're not just clocking in to complete a task. You're building something that actually matters. And that? That's power worth protecting.

Remember: **The surge is the signal.**

So, when you feel it, even for a second, mark that sh*t. Trace it. Study it. Build around it. Because that's your signal. That's what pulls the pointer on your compass. That's the moment you stop chasing outside validation because the work is already paying you back. In goosebumps. In grins. In a flow of energy that can't be faked. That's your body and soul telling you, *More of this, please.*

Forget the vanity metrics. Forget the algorithms. Forget what your competitors are doing. Forget external validation. Forget trying to be impressive.

The best metric for great work is whether it makes you feel something.

Ask yourself one thing: *Does this give me goosebumps?* If the answer is yes, you've tapped into your real power source. If the answer is no, maybe it's time to rewire some sh*t.

At the end of the day, your best work isn't the most polished. It's the most alive. So, don't just chase the success. Chase the surge. That's where the real power lives.

And if it gives you goosebumps, don't be surprised when the world follows.

RULE 15

YOUR BUSINESS IS NOT YOUR IDENTITY

YOU ARE NOT YOUR STRIPE DASHBOARD, SWEETHEART

YOUR BUSINESS IS NOT YOUR IDENTITY

Let's start with a hard truth wrapped in love: **Your business is something you run, not something you are.**

Read that again. Slowly. Tattoo it on a soft spot that takes a bit longer to heal.

If you're anything like most of us who've built something from scratch, you've made this fatal mistake:

- » You didn't just build a business. You built a mirror. And then you stared into it so long, you started believing it was you.
- » You are not your quarterly revenue. You are not the size of your following. You are not your open rates, your engagement stats, or the dumb comment some troll left on a Google review.
- » You are not your logo. You are not your "voice." You are not your positioning deck.
- » You are not your inbox, your invoices, your calendar, or your business name printed in a fancy serif font.

You are you. A person. A soul. A living, breathing, laughing, flawed, growing human being who just so happens to run a business, not become it. And if that sounds like a subtle difference . . . it's not.

It's the difference between freedom and emotional servitude. Between burnout and longevity. Between building something great and being consumed by it.

WHEN DID WE START BELIEVING THAT ACHIEVEMENT = IDENTITY?

Probably somewhere between "follow your passion" and "monetize everything you love."

I started as a production designer. Then, I was an art director. Then, a creative director. I built a team. Then a brand. Then a business. Then, I became the business. And suddenly, when sales were down, I felt like sh*t. When a project fell apart, it was my character on the chopping block. When a client ghosted me, it wasn't just annoying; it was personal.

Sound familiar?

You didn't start a business. You accidentally became it.

HEALTHY ENTREPRENEURS BUILD HEALTHY BUSINESSES. BURNED-OUT ENTREPRENEURS BUILD BITTERNESS WITH A LOGO.

But here's the truth no one talks about: **You can be proud of your work and still be separate from it.** You can be passionate without being consumed. You can care deeply without letting it become your identity. Because the moment your self-worth depends on your business metrics? You've given the keys to your joy to a Google Sheet with a budget. And that, my friend, is the opposite of freedom.

MAKE SPACE FOR THE YOU WHO DOESN'T CREATE ON COMMAND

There's a version of you who's not on a deadline. Who doesn't care about feedback forms or pitch decks or onboarding workflows. There's a version of you who's softer. Who reads for fun. Who laughs mid-sentence. Who sits in silence and doesn't need to produce anything to feel worthy of existing.

That version of you deserves to breathe, so make room for it. That version is not a liability. It's the battery pack for your business.

Because if your ideas and creativity become a factory, your soul will burn out like a fluorescent bulb in a Waffle House. Healthy entrepreneurs build healthy businesses. Burned-out entrepreneurs build bitterness with a logo.

So, rest. Unplug. Stop tying your value to what you're producing this week. You're not a product. You're a person.

YOUR BUSINESS DOESN'T DESERVE YOUR WHOLE IDENTITY

It deserves your excellence. It deserves your attention. It deserves your strategy, your vision, your care. But not your self-worth. Not your weekends. Not your entire identity like a hostage held by client deliverables.

LET YOUR BUSINESS BE THE VEHICLE, NOT THE VERDICT.

Your business deserves your best, but it doesn't deserve *EVERY OUNCE* of you. **Do not give it your peace.** Because when the business hits a dip (and it will), and your identity is glued to it, you won't just feel like things are hard. **You'll feel like you're failing as a person.**

You are not the job title you gave yourself (as creative as it may sound). You are more. You're just a human having a human experience. Running a thing that is allowed to wobble. That's called *life*. And the more you remember that, the better everything gets.

DETACH TO SOAR

The second you stop needing your business to be your entire personality is the moment you finally breathe again.

» You'll stop obsessing over the numbers.
» You'll stop comparing yourself to everyone on the internet.
» You'll stop making reactive decisions just to feel in control.
» You'll lead better. Live better. And love the damn work again.

Let your business be the vehicle, not the verdict.

You are not here to be profitable. You are here to be whole. And the world needs that version of you more than it needs another email campaign or Q3 projection.

So, step back. Step out. And remember: **You were valuable long before you had an LLC.**

YOU DON'T NEED A SABBATICAL—YOU NEED TO FEEL SOMETHING AGAIN

Success doesn't come from absence. It comes from presence. From getting back in the ring. From doing the work that feels like you. From cutting out all the tasks, tactics, and people that don't align with the reason you ever started.

So, if your business feels like it's lost its soul, maybe it's time to start running it like a human again. Not a robot. Not a brand archetype.

Not a KPI machine. A human. With a heartbeat. With a spark. With something to say.

Let's not forget—you didn't build this thing to survive. You built it to feel. To create. To light sh*t up. So, get back to the work that reminds you why you still give a damn. That's where the real power is. Not in your process, not in your positioning, but in the passion you still carry. You just have to stop burying it beneath all the bullsh*t.

Reignite the thing that made you dangerous in the first place—your passion. That's your pulse. That's your edge. That's your legacy.

And when you find that pulse again? Run with it like hell.

CONCLUSION

HOLD THESE TRUTHS

READ THIS OUT LOUD IF YOU FORGOT WHO THE HELL YOU ARE

By now, you know the deal.

This book was never about business tactics. It was a manifesto. A wake-up call wrapped in expletives and truth serum. A reminder that you didn't come this far just to build something you resent. So, let's end with the truths we've been building toward all along.

We hold these truths to be self-evident:

- That **you are not your business**, and your worth cannot be measured in retainer contracts or retweets.
- That **boundaries are not a luxury.** They are the blueprint for longevity, peace, and creative freedom.
- That **you are allowed to say no without explanation** because "no" is a complete sentence, not a missed opportunity.
- That **passion beats perfection every time**, and messy, human, soulful work will always outlast sterile, over-polished garbage.
- That **you can run a business without becoming a martyr** to it.
- That **you do not need to prove your value.** You just need to believe it.
- That **rest is not weakness.** Slowness is not failure. Hustle is not a god.
- That **relationships matter more than deliverables.** And who you work with is just as important as what you create.

- » That **everything is an experiment.** And failure is simply proof that you had the balls to try.
- » That **you attract what you are.** So, be intentional with your energy. It's the loudest thing in the room.
- » That **your gut is smarter than your fear.** Trust it. Move with it. Build by it.
- » That **kindness is not a weakness.** It's a filter. A razor-sharp one.

If this book did its job, you're not walking away with a fifteen-point checklist. You're walking away with a new standard. A louder voice inside your gut. A sharper line between "enough" and "too much." A little more fire. A lot more peace.

You don't need more business advice. You need your own damn permission. To be bold. To be messy. To be kind and powerful at the same time. To build something meaningful and still have a life you enjoy.

That's the point of all of this. Not to hustle harder. But to come home to yourself in your business, in your relationships, and in every decision you make from here on out.

Because if you're going to build a business from scratch, if you're going to put your heart and soul on the line, if you're going to show up day after day and give a damn, then you deserve to build it your way.

- » So, write your rules.
- » Draw your line.
- » Charge your worth.
- » Protect your peace.
- » Work with people who get it.
- » **Set the tone and hold your *SAVAGE STANDARDS*.**
- » And let everything else burn.

So, go on. Build the business you love. And watch what happens when the universe meets you halfway.

ONE FINAL THOUGHT: THE "WHY" THAT WON'T LEAVE ME ALONE

Whether playing with building blocks as a child. Or putting pencil to paper in art class. Or practicing graphic design all of my career. From Legos to logos, I've been creative my whole life. Which means I've been a bit of a chaos wrangler, a dream builder, a last-minute miracle worker, and occasionally . . . a caffeinated wreck behind a laptop.

But through all the years, the late nights, the burnout cycles, and the hundredth round of feedback, I kept asking myself the same questions: *Why do I keep doing this? Why do I keep showing up, pouring my heart into pixels, copy, campaigns, and concepts? Why do I burn hours crafting beauty for people who don't always notice? Why do I stay when 80 percent of this job feels like it's built from admin hell and emotional labor?*

And then it hit me.

The 20 percent makes the rest of it worth it.

It's not just about balance. It's about meaning. And for me, the meaning lives in that one sacred space: **The words that affirm who I am.**

That's it. That's the secret. My personal fuel. My creative oxygen. That childlike hunger to hear:

"This is amazing."

"Holy crap . . . you nailed it."

"Damn . . . that's really awesome."

Strip everything else away—the client briefs, the project scopes, the timelines, the invoices—and what's left? A kid who just wants to make something cool and hear, "You did great."

It's not about ego. It's about connection. Because when someone sees what you made, what you pulled out of thin air, and says, "Yes. That." It hits your soul like a tuning fork.

That's the stuff that feeds me. That's the thing that keeps me up late and gets me up early. That 20 percent where something comes alive, where I remember, *Oh, yeah, this is what I'm built for.*

WE'RE ALL WIRED FOR IT

The truth is this: **We're all driven by something simple.** Something primal. Some core need that never really grows up. Maybe for you, it's being seen. Maybe it's proving someone wrong. Maybe it's control in a chaotic world. Maybe it's the thrill of making something that didn't exist yesterday.

Whatever it is, you've got one.

And if you don't make space to find it? If you stay buried in the to-do lists, the team drama, the launch pressure, and the constant inbox war . . . you'll forget. You'll lose the joy. You'll burn the fuse down and wonder why it all feels numb.

So, here's your challenge: **Go find your "why."** The one thing that actually feeds you. Name it. Claim it. Build around it. Because once you know that spark—really know it—you can design your entire business, your calendar, your energy, your creativity, and your future to protect it like your favorite flame.

And when you do? Everything, even the 80 percent, starts to make a little more sense.

It's about the pure joy of finding your place in it all. Building something you'll be proud of. And making your mark that lasts long after you're gone.

Cheers.

Savagestandards.com